Many Prophets One Wisdom

Global Values for Getting Along

Phil Thompson

Manor House

Many Prophets, One Wisdom

Library and Archives Canada
Cataloguing in Publication

Thompson, Phil, 1956-
Many prophets, one wisdom : global values for getting along / Phil Thompson.

Includes bibliographical references.

ISBN: 978-1-897453-67-4

1. Conduct of life. 2. Interpersonal relations--Religious aspects. 3. Prophets--History. I. Title.

BJ1595.T56 2010   170'.44   C2010-907094-1

Printed and bound in Canada

First Edition.
144 pages.
All rights reserved.

Cover design: Michael B. Davie and Donovan Davie

Published October 30, 2010
Manor House Publishing Inc.

We gratefully acknowledge the financial support of the Government of Canada through Book Fund Canada, Dept. of Canadian Heritage.

Manor House Publishing Inc.
www.manor-house.biz
905-648-2193

The Prophets:

The Rig-Veda, The Upanishads, The Pali Canon and *The Bhagavad-Gita* (Indian Subcontinent, Hinduism, Buddhism); *Confucius* and *Lao Tzu* (China); *The Torah, The Gospels, The Qur'an and The Forty Hadith* (Monotheists, Judaism, Christianity, Islam); works of *John Locke, Jean-Jacques Rousseau, Adam Smith, John Stuart Mill* and *Karl Marx and Friederich Engels* (Western Liberal Democracy, Secular Humanists, Western Atheists).

The Prophets' Global Values for Getting Along

Three sacrifices: freedom, wealth and violence.

Six values: tolerance, self-reflection, humility, compassion, inclusiveness and reciprocity.

Five vices: greed, violence, ignorance, dogmatism and exclusivity.

Deeds speak: behaviour matters, hypocrisy, leadership and equanimity.

The Inspiration

For wisdom, listen not to me but to the Word, and know that all is one.

Heraclitus (535 – 475 BCE)

Everywhere new technology and communications brings men and nations closer together, the concerns of one inevitably become the concerns of all. And our new closeness is stripping away the false masks, the illusion of differences which is at the root of injustice and hate and war.

Senator Robert F. Kennedy, 1966

People, I just want to say, you know, can we all get along?

Rodney King, 1992

Acknowledgements

Thank you to all the publishers and translators listed in the bibliography for preserving and passing on the works of these great thinkers,

And thank you to Michael Davie of Manor House Publishing for remembering, encouraging and guiding.

*For Mathew, Michael, Cameron, Kristen and Theresa,
Their future is the purpose for my present.*

* * * * *

Table of Contents

Foreward	9
Introduction	11
Chapter 1 - Rodney King's Question	15
Chapter 2 - Fourteen Prophets	21
Chapter 3 - Three Sacrifices	31
Chapter 4 - Six Values	49
Chapter 5 – Deeds Speak	77
Chapter 6 - Five Vices	97
Chapter 7 - The Prophets on Enemies	115
Chapter 8 - What Really Matters	125
Chapter 9 - The Common Works of Humankind	133
Bibliography	141
About the Author	143

Foreword

By **Michael B Davie**

"People, I just want to say, you know, can we all get along?"

That question, was posed by African American Rodney King following race riots sparked by his videotaped unprovoked beating by police.

It's a simple yet compelling question that continues to resonate in today's world of global conflicts and strife. Can our world find common ground to live together in mutual respect and harmony? Can we all get along?

Lawyer-philosopher **Phil Thompson** explores that question in considerable detail in his remarkable and insightful book ***Many Prophets, One Wisdom***.

Thompson has studied the teachings of our greatest prophets from varied cultures, nations and religions. All these prophets find enormous value and merit in peaceful coexistence with others.

Collectively the prophets' words of wisdom provide common values and attitudes that cross time and ideology and can guide humanity toward a world free of the wars and conflicts that have been so costly in terms of loss of life, freedom, dignity, and hope.

As Thompson notes: "The revelation is that our prophets have far more in common than many of us might realize; that we share one planet; that we are and can be one people."

What is needed is for whole states to embrace this "oneness" and engage in international relations that go beyond self-interest to include the interests of the other party in forging win-win arrangements that respect the needs of citizens of every nation.

But change begins at an individual level, and here, Thompson provides personal examples and anecdotes to illustrate how this peaceful concept applies at street level.

Governments, after all, are composed of politicians who are for the most part ordinary people with the same needs as all of us. If individual politicians the world over can embrace such positive global values for getting along, those values will inevitably be reflected in government policies and approaches towards treating their own citizens – and those of other nations – with respect and dignity and compassion.

It all begins with you and I and grows to encompass everyone. We must all embrace the timeless value of getting along with others for the benefit of ourselves, our nations, our planet.

Many Prophets, One Wisdom is truly a book whose time has come. It could not possibly be any more needed and timely. This is the way to move forward to the next level of tolerance and understanding, the way to advance the globalization of human values via the teachings of some of our greatest prophets.

- **Michael B Davie**, author, *Winning Ways*

Introduction

On March 3rd, 1991 Rodney King was speeding down Interstate 210 in California. He was chased by the California Highway Patrol for eight miles before pulling over. His arrest turned violent, and several police officers were video-taped beating him. This event received worldwide media attention.

Rodney King was an African American. His community perceived this to be an all too common indication of race-based abuse by the Los Angeles police force.

The police officers involved were charged, but then acquitted at a trial that took place outside Los Angeles County. The only people on the jury where white, Asian or Latino.

The verdict triggered massive riots in Los Angeles that lasted three days, resulting in many deaths and injuries as well as hundreds of millions of dollars in property damage.

On the third day of the riots Rodney King appeared on television appealing for calm and pleading for peace. At that time he posed a question for the ages: *"People, I just want to say, you know, can we all get along?"*

His question stuck with me for years, especially when asked in its negative – People, why *can't* we get along?

A few years after the Rodney King incident I held a business meeting in my office with two clients and their accountant. The clients were farmers and adherents of Sikhism, a religion founded in the 15th century CE in India by the prophet Guru Nanek Dev, the first of ten Sikh gurus. Their accountant was an Ismaili Muslim born in East Africa, educated in England and now living and working in Canada. Being a Muslim, his prophet was Muhammad, the Arab spiritual leader who founded Islam around 610 CE. Being Ismaili, he was a Shiite Muslim whose community leader is known to the world as the Aga Khan. Then there was me, a Canadian-born lawyer. I went to the Anglican Church as a child but my primary prophet at the time of this meeting was probably John Stuart Mill, an English philosopher who lived in the 19th century.

As is not uncommon in my part of the world four people from three different ideologies and with three geographically varied family histories had come together in one place at the same time to solve a problem faced by one of them. However they did so as equals, with a feeling of mutual trust and respect. This is something many Canadians take for granted, perhaps too much for granted. It is not as common in the rest of the world as we would like it to be.

The idea occurred to me during this meeting that many of us have a central prophet or leading voice from a specific point in time that has had a great deal of influence in our lives. It also occurred to me that we often fail to heed or respect the prophets who came before or after this leading voice. As if our favoured prophet cornered the market on common sense and righteous living not just in his or her own time but for all time. I began to wonder why some of us just stop listening. I wondered why some of us get carried away by the teachings of one prophet to the exclusion of all others, even a prophet who lived thousands of years ago in a far away land and time.

I have always been struck by the lyric fragment "idolatry of ideology" in the Bruce Cockburn song *They Call It Democracy*. The questions coming to me during this meeting brought this lyric to mind. Some of us become so in enthralled with our own ideas that we can justify almost any action in their name. It is to humankind's ongoing discredit that many of us prefer conflict, bloodshed, destruction and inhumanity to simply softening the way we think about things.

I also realized how ignorant I was of the teachings of prophets from other philosophies. I felt this was an issue I could only address by reading those prophets for myself in their own words. That I would have to see for myself what differences there were between their teachings, and whether there was any commonality we could build on if we really wanted to.

With the demise of the Iron Curtain in 1989 and the development of capitalism in China I had assumed humanity was about to enter a new era of peaceful development, one without ideology based violence. After all, hadn't state monitored capitalism and secular democracy won out both politically and economically? Didn't all religions teach tolerance and non-violence? Weren't we all now moving in the same general direction?

Then 9/11 and the War on Terror happened. It looked like conflict based on ideology had not left us for very long, if it left us at all. Rodney King's question seemed as important as ever, as did Bruce Cockburn's idea of idolatry of ideology. I decided it was time I looked into the issue of "getting along" and what I could learn about it from reading important works from our leading prophets

This book is the result of my inquiry.

I originally wrote this manuscript for myself, as I learn best when I write about what I am learning. Writing helps me crystallize my thinking and commit things to memory.

I have a different motivation in publishing this book, however. I am not a philosopher or an academic. My goal in publishing this manuscript is not to teach but to encourage everyone to learn for themselves, and in doing so to learn more about themselves, their communities, and the larger global community. I learned a great deal from reading our leading prophets and philosophers in their own words. I hope others will do the same.

1 Rodney King's Question

"People, I just want to say, you know, can we all get along?" Rodney King asked this question in 1992. Being able to answer *"Yes"* to this question is more important than ever.

The convergence of an exploding population and technological change is re-shaping globalization from an economic to a social force. Our countries are not homogenous forts we can hide within. The cost of being left behind by an advancing world is a price none of us should be willing to pay ourselves or be content to witness in others.

Globalization has been a force to unite the world in a single economy. Now it is becoming a force to unite us in a common way of life. We need to secure this way of life with common values that bridge old religions, politics and ideologies without replacing them. We need to articulate global values that provide the "how" and "why" we are able to get along on an increasingly crowded, dirty and interconnected planet. We need to define common personal beliefs that end war and reduce conflict for everyone, not just the rich and powerful.

To be effective, accepted and sustained, global values must emerge from and resonate within the billions of ordinary people who live in this world. Global values have to be a bottom up phenomenon. We have seen what happens when values, beliefs and ideology are left to the few and the powerful to define and implement – hundreds of years of war, violence, misery and suffering, the burden of which falls on ordinary people far more than it falls on the ideological elites that often ignite the passions of conflict to begin with.

Over the last three hundred years political power has increasingly devolved to ordinary people. The basis of political power has been changing from ownership of land and military power to support from and accountability to ordinary people.

Economic power has been changing as well, from the ability to coerce the labour of ordinary people to the ability to attract and retain their spending power. In economics as in politics the power of the many is eclipsing the power of the few. It is time for this trend to apply to beliefs as well. We need ordinary people to take power over global beliefs, just as they have taken and continue to acquire political and economic power.

There is a common goodness that pervades ordinary life throughout the world. This common goodness stubbornly survives our most insane efforts to crush it. We need ordinary people to define the common goodness so often experienced on a day-to-day basis, and make it the standard by which political, economic and ideological leaders are held accountable.

Most of us can barely articulate the basis for our own beliefs, however. And we are often ill-equipped to understand, debate or integrate the beliefs of others. We spend too much time pointing out or debating differences in beliefs and not enough time identifying what they already have in common. This ignorance often nourishes the roots of our most profound conflicts and prejudices.

I went looking for wisdom concerning these matters in the teachings of our collective prophets. After all, their teachings have had meaning for billions of people and in some cases for thousands of years. I wanted to see what they had in common. I expected they would say something profound about what we need to believe and what we need to do in order to get along in a modern world. I hoped they would contain a collective wisdom that could speak to ordinary people across time, place, heritage and ideology.

I purchased English language versions of the original works of the prophets that seemed most influential in today's religious and political climate: *The Rig-Veda, The Upanishads, The Pali Canon* and *The Bhagavad-Gita* (Indian Subcontinent, Hinduism, Buddhism); *Confucius* and *Lao Tzu* (China); *The Torah, The Gospels* and *The Qur'an* (Monotheists, Judaism, Christianity, Islam); and works of *John Locke, Jean-Jacques Rousseau, Adam Smith, John Stuart Mill* and *Karl Marx and Friederich Engels* (Western Liberal Democracy, Secular Humanists, Western Atheists). I read them all, looking for the teachings of these prophets in their own words. I looked for what they had to say about living together and getting along.

What I found was a common wisdom for dealing with my neighbours and friends in our connected and multicultural world. I learned that a common set of beliefs, values and observations for avoiding conflict and living in peace already exists. I learned that we have done a poor job of following them. I developed a deeper understanding of the ideological similarities that link us together, no matter what our ideological base. I found a common sense of what really matters.

With the entire knowledge of the human race available at our fingertips almost instantly accessing knowledge and information is not the problem it once was. However, knowing which voices to listen to, which voices to tune out, and which ideas to take to heart is becoming harder than ever.

What I learned in reading our leading prophets was good news. Over thousands of years much hard thinking has already been done. If we return to the roots of our beliefs and pool our collective wisdom we can articulate a simple common wisdom that crosses time, geography and ideology.

We can articulate a collective, global philosophy for getting along. It may take sacrifice for us to hear it, but it is a sacrifice we need to make if we are going to survive the challenges of the modern age.

This teaching contains three great sacrifices – freedom, wealth and violence.

It includes six universal values for getting along – tolerance, self-reflection, humility, compassion, inclusiveness and reciprocity.

It defines five universal vices that can keep us from getting along – greed, violence, ignorance, dogmatism and exclusivity.

And it teaches us that behaviour matters, that what we do is far more important than what we say, and that the attitude we bring to our actions is just as important as the actions themselves.

The revelation is that our prophets have far more in common than many of us might realize; that we share one planet; that we are and can be one people.

Not that this wisdom is the final answer to all our problems for all time. It is only the starting point for a meaningful discussion of the global values we need to define and adopt if we are going to end the conflict and misery that has been part of the human condition for all too long.

While the wisdom of the prophets referred to in this book has a lot to say about what it takes to get along in our modern world, it is not a comprehensive answer to all the ecological, biomedical, technological and ethical questions coming our way in ever increasing numbers. How could it be? This wisdom is collected from the teachings of long dead prophets, many of whom could never have imagined a planet with billions of people, able to communicate instantly across thousands of miles with text, voice and image, and with the ability to quickly and easily destroy millions of people and mountains of other life by design or accident.

The teachings of these prophets are presented in their own words so you can read them for yourself, challenge any conclusions I may have come to, decide for yourself whether there is commonality or discordance, and come to your own conclusions on what their teachings can or should mean in your community and our wider world.

Ultimately this book is about choice. The choice we have to end whatever ignorance or prejudice we have about our own worldview and the worldviews of others. The choice we have to pull from our own beliefs those values that are most consistent with the beliefs of others and most conducive to living in a peaceful and prosperous world. The choice we have to soften or surrender values that promote or lead to conflict. The choice we have as individuals, families, communities and nations to select not only our values, but to work with others to choose the values for our planet as a whole.

This book throws open the question of what it takes to simply getting along. It is an enquiry that has no end. New challenges are guaranteed to arise that require us to revisit what it takes to get along.

Global population growth, along with its corresponding environmental impact, is just such a challenge. It is also an enquiry as long as each lifetime, as every person faces the challenge of getting along at a personal level from their very first to their very last steps.

We cannot help defining the world we live in. Everything we think, say and do, does that for us. Today we have an opportunity, need and obligation to recognize and implement a common global wisdom more so than at any other time in our collective history.

There seems no better place to start than with the collective wisdom of our most enduring and influential prophets.

2 - Fourteen Prophets

Wisdom by Aggregation

If we put fourteen people in a room and asked them to consider the problems of the world they would bring fourteen different perspectives, especially if they came from fourteen different cultures. If we asked them to tell us what it takes to get along in the modern world they would each have suggestions to make, reflecting the principles they grew up with and their life experiences so far.

It seems impossible, however, that everyone in the group would produce the same suggestions. They might not even unanimously agree on any one idea for getting along. On the other hand, it does seem pretty likely that a consensus would develop. That we could collect and collate their suggestions into a single, common wisdom of what really matters when it comes to answering Rodney King's question. This collective wisdom would be even more significant if these fourteen people represented some of the wisest and most influential thinkers in today's world. It is this collective wisdom that I went looking for.

Everyone has a view of the world and how to get along in it. It is often subconscious and cultural. Something so obvious and taken for granted that nothing else is conceivable. However, our worldviews all have something in common. At their root, often in some distant past that most of us have not investigated, a "prophet" gave that worldview a significant voice. It may have splintered in different directions in subsequent decades or centuries. It may have been adopted by some and rejected by others. It may have been debated, changed, adapted or warped. But somewhere back there are the original words of a influential thinker whose ideas have become so basic to some modern society that they are accepted almost without question. These are the prophets that I had to read for myself.

Choosing the Prophets

My first issue was to decide which prophets to read. The Oxford English Dictionary defines "prophet" as both "an inspired teacher or proclaimer of the word of God" and "a person who advocates a new belief or theory." This definition was the touchstone I used to decide who to read now and who to set aside for another day.

It also seemed appropriate to me to consider key political prophets, as well as the most obvious religious ones, as current conflicts seem to include elements of both politics and religion.

I was also primarily interested in prophets with significant contemporary influence. My interest was to understand the time and place in which I am living. This was not going to be a historical enquiry but an attempt to understand my friends and neighbours in the worldwide, internet, multi-media and air travel connected world in which I live.

My interest was not the greatest prophets of all time, or even the wisest or most profound, but those that seemed to hold sway in my world at this time.

Shear numbers seemed to be a good place to start. According to The Economist Pocket World in Figures 2006

Edition, China (population 1.304 billion in 2003 and projected 1.3902 billion in 2050) and India (population 1.065 billion in 2003 and projected 1.563 billion in 2050) seemed pretty obvious areas of influence.

The U.S., being the world's third largest country by population and an economy roughly 2.5 times the size of next biggest economy ($10.947 trillion versus Japan at $4.300 trillion), also seemed an easy choice of study.

I also considered the world's religions, especially those with the largest number of adherents, namely Christianity (2.1 billion), Islam (1.3 billion), Hinduism (900 million), Traditional Chinese (394 million) and Buddhism (376 million).

Finally, I considered the political and economic theories that seemed to have survived the ideological purges of the 20th century. In the spring of 2007 the success of European liberal democracies and free-market economies seemed undeniable.

However, Communism and Socialism were still a major tug on the conscience of freewheeling competition as the basis of society.

While this list will undoubtedly have its critics, I decided I would have a pretty good understanding of the most influential prophets of the current era if I read and considered the following: *The Rig-Vida, The Upanishads, The Bhagavad-Gita* and *The Pali Canon* (Indian Subcontinent, Hinduism, Buddhism); *Confucius* and *Lao Tzu* (traditional China); *The Torah, The Christian Gospels* and *The Qur'an* (Monotheists, Judaism, Christianity, Islam); and *John Locke, Jean-Jacques Rousseau, Adam Smith, John Stuart Mill* and *Karl Marx and Friederich Engels* (European Liberal Democracy, Secular Humanists,

Modern Atheists). This became my list of prophets and their teachings became the subject of my reflections.

Of course this is far from an exhaustive list. There are many other worthy and influential prophets in our collective past. However, the practical realities of time and space forced me to limit this inquiry to a number that can be readily worked with. I believe the prophets chosen here are widely representative and a good base for a broader enquiry of other prophets not included.

It was important for me to read the teachings of these prophets in their own words without interpretation or filter. This need seemed particularly important for this project as there are so many different interpretations of these prophets at work in the world today.

I could not read all the teachings of all the prophets as they were originally taught. In many cases all we have are fragmented records of oral traditions from ancient languages no longer used. The original words of the prophets were often not recorded at the time they were spoken. In some cases the very existence of the prophet as a historical person outside the oral history of his teachings cannot be proven.

In many cases there are no original versions of the first written record of the teachings in the original languages. We have translations of translations. On top of all that, I am not a linguist. All I could do was find what appeared to be relatively honest English translations of original works, which themselves may have been translations.

I wanted to know what the prophets had to say about how we should be living together in peace. I wanted to know what ideas they had in common. I wanted to see if there was a simple, common wisdom that could resonate with many peoples of many different backgrounds, languages and cultures; a wisdom that could prove useful and meaningful across long periods of time. I wanted to have a basis to compare practice and theory.

What follows in this Chapter is the briefest outline of where these works came from and who these prophets were. However, there is no substitute for reading these works for yourself. They are readily available in libraries, bookstores or on-line. They are some of the most influential works in recorded history. They are challenging, beautiful, complex, simple and contradictory, just like the people and cultures that produced them and just like the people and cultures that try to work with them today.

The Rig-Veda

The Rig-Veda is a collection of hymns of praise to various gods and is considered one of the oldest and most sacred Hindu texts. Its origins are lost in antiquity and are the subject of some debate. Some Hindu scholars have claimed they represent a tradition of 8,000 to 12,000 years.

More skeptical scholars have placed their age at 2,000 to 1,200 BCE, which still makes them 4,000 to 3,000 years old. Whatever their age, they are a moving insight into our early spirituality and our inevitable and powerful connection to the Earth and nature.

The Upanishads

The Upanishads are a later collection of sacred Hindu texts, commonly associated with the period around 800 to 400 BCE. They contain sacred teaching from a variety of sources. Upanishad is a word associated with the Sanskrit word for "sitting near," as in sitting at the feet of a master.

While the Rig-Veda looks outward into the natural world for a deeper understanding of Mankind and its connections within the universe, the Upanishads look within each person for the source of this connection. Like many other spiritual texts, the Upanishads are a collection of dozens of spiritual treatises assembled together. They contain beautiful and poetic images of love, peace and harmony.

The Bhagavad-Gita

The Bhagavad-Gita is an epic poem in eighteen chapters. It is the most famous of Hindu religious texts. Its written legacy is most commonly dated around the 1st to 2nd century CE, or about the time that the Christian Gospels were being written.

Its oral legacy, however, is much debated, and the poem could be as old as the 6th century BCE.

The Pali Canon

The Pali Canon is a major text in Buddhist philosophy. The Canon's written tradition appears to date from around the 1st century BCE, when it was originally recorded in the Pali language in what is now Sri Lanka.

Its oral tradition, however, appears to date from the 5th to 3rd centuries BCE, or just after the death of Siddhartha Gotama, the founder of Buddhism. The Pali Canon contains the recollections of Gotama's disciples as to various teachings made by him during his ministry.

Confucius

Kong Fuzi, for Master Kong, and known in the West as Confucius, was an itinerant teacher and philosopher during the 6th and 5th century BCE (551 to 479 BCE). His particular interest was government and leadership. It is unlikely that anyone in history has been able to compress as much wisdom into a single sentence.

His teaching has come down to us through various works, including the Analects of Confucius, recorded by his disciples after his death.

Lao Tzu

The philosophy known as Taoism, or Daoism, is credited to a fifth century BCE Chinese philosopher named Lao Tzu, or Laozi. The major work of Taoism is the Tao te ching, or Dao de jing, a collection of teachings in eighty-one chapters and recorded in the 3rd century BCE.

The Tao te ching is the shortest of the philosophical works considered in this project, and can be the most difficult to fit into a logical framework, which presumably is an essential element of Tao in and of itself. Tao te ching means "The Book of the Way and Its Power".

The Torah

The Torah is the holiest of the Jewish religious texts. It contains five books – Genesis, Exodus, Leviticus, Numbers and Deuteronomy – which are also the first five books of the Christian Old Testament.

The oral tradition of the Torah is debated, with estimates from 1,200 BCE to 600 BCE being quite common.

The written tradition is also debated, with estimates commonly in the range of 400 BCE to 100 BCE.

The Gospels

The Gospels are the first four books of the New Testament in the Christian Bible, and consist of the books known as Matthew, Mark, Luke and John. They record the life and ministry of Jesus of Nazareth, and purport to contain the teachings of Jesus in his own words.

We know with certainty that the oral and written tradition of the Gospels date from the 1st and 2nd century CE and they were written some years after the death of Jesus.

The Qur'an and Forty Hadith

The Qur'an, also referred to as the Koran, is the holy scripture of Islam. It contains the word of God as revealed to the prophet Muhammad, who lived in the Arabian Peninsula from 570 to 632 CE.

Muhammad's ministry commenced in 610 CE and continued until his death. The Qur'an contains the word of God as revealed to him and passed on to his followers in their oral tradition. It was assembled in written form some years after his death. The Hadith are complementary to the Qur'an, and also purport to contain teachings of Muhammad in his own words.

John Locke

John Locke was an English doctor and philosopher. He lived from 1632 to 1704. His two works considered here, Two Treatises of Government and A Letter Concerning Toleration, were both published in 1689. They were written following years of civil and political religious strife within England and England's experiment with a republican government.

Jean-Jacques Rousseau

Jean-Jacques Rousseau was a French writer and philosopher who lived from 1712 to 1778. In 1762 he published The Social Contract, the work considered here. His book foreshadowed the American Revolution of 1776, the French Revolution of 1789, and the social upheavals in 19th century Europe.

Adam Smith

Adam Smith was a Scottish academic and philosopher, who lived from 1723 to 1790. He published An Inquiry into the Wealth of Nations in 1776 and launched not only the field of modern economics but provided the economic counterpoint to the religious, social and political restructuring emanating from Europe at the time.

He is considered a prophet of modern capitalism, although many capitalists might be surprised what they will find in the Wealth of Nations if they read it for themselves.

John Stuart Mill

John Stuart Mill was an English philosopher. He lived from 1806 to 1873. His seminal work for the purposes of this book is On Liberty, a lengthy essay published in 1859 that reflects on the limitations which should be imposed on the power of society over the rights of the individual.

Karl Marx and Friederich Engels

Karl Marx (1818 to 1883) and his patron and collaborator Friederich Engels (1820 to 1895) are modern prophets of collectivism. Together they wrote the Communist Manifesto, published in 1848. They also collaborated on

Das Kapital, Marx's seminal critique on political economy, written by Marx, edited by Engels, and published by Engels in England in 1885, after the death of Marx.

Their Collective Voice

These, then, are the fourteen prophets I assembled, aggregated and considered for this book.

What follows is my interpretation of their collective voice for getting along in our modern world. I do not offer this interpretation as a definitive answer to Rodney King's question, but as a catalyst for ongoing discussion. Nor do I offer this interpretation as a substitute for anyone reading these and other prophets for themselves.

The onus is on each of us who wishes to live in a world free of conflict to think about, advocate and act upon those values which, over time, consistently lead to a more peaceful and prosperous world, not just for ourselves but for everyone else as well.

3 Three Sacrifices

The idea of sacrifice is a common thread running through these teachings. It is an idea as old as the Rig-Veda and as recent as Karl Marx. It can be traditional, as in the animal sacrifices of the oldest texts; or contemporary, as in the surrender of natural freedom referred to in the most recent works considered here.

The Rig-Veda, the Upanishads and the Bhagavad-Gita all call for sacrifice as a way to receive benefit from the Gods or to find God in a spiritual way.

The Pali Canon asks us to identify and detach from the things to which we are most attached as part of a spiritual journey to inner peace and happiness.

Sacrifice is all-pervasive in monotheism. The very word Islam means surrender, as in surrendering to the will of God, a unifying principle among Jews, Christians and Muslims. In the Torah, God's ultimate test of Abraham's worthiness is Abraham's willingness to sacrifice his son at God's request. In Christianity, the entire life and death of Jesus is a sacrifice for the benefit of humankind.

In the Chinese traditions, Confucius supports ritual sacrifices to ancestors, as well as the broader requirement of obedience and service to ones parents, elder siblings and sovereign. Finally, modern Western democratic prophets unite around the idea that society's security as a whole requires a surrendering of natural individual freedoms.

The Upanishads contain a beautiful expression of the spirit of sacrifice:

God is found in the soul when sought with truth and self-sacrifice, as fire is found in wood, water in hidden springs, cream in milk, and oil in the oil fruit. There is a Spirit who is hidden in all things, as cream is hidden in milk, and who is the source of all self-knowledge and self-sacrifice. This is Brahman, the Spirit Supreme. (Upanishads, Svetasvatara Upanishad, Part I)

When it comes to getting along, and considering sacrifice in the context of Rodney King's question, these prophets have collectively identified three key sacrifices: freedom, wealth and violence.

We must be willing to trade our individual entitlement to freedom, wealth and violence in return for participation in collective security, prosperity and peace. In the modern world we must do this as individuals, and also as communities, nations and countries.

Freedom: The First Sacrifice

Whether it is called worship, obedience, surrender, the Way, the Dao or the rule of law, there is a strong consensus among these prophets that we each must sacrifice a large part of our individual freedom to do what we want when we want in order to get along in a peaceful society.

This idea seems to be at the very root of society itself, and is built on the belief, sometimes spiritual and sometimes commonsense, that there are forces, principles or realities bigger than our individual lives that we must accept if we are going to find shelter within meaningful societies.

A good place to begin demonstrating this idea is with the prophets who helped found modern Western Liberal Democracy. "Freedom" has been the war cry of "the West" for several hundred years, and is as strident in some places today as it ever was.

However, freedom is not absolute. The partial suppression of individual liberty is a key element in the creation of all societies including democratic ones. This can be seen in how we live in the West today. It can be argued that our modern Western countries are among the least "free" in the history of humankind. Our law books mushroom in size each year with new and more complex regulations that intrude into every aspect of modern living. The more we work to bring security, fairness, honesty and respect into our societies, the more law it takes to accomplish those goals. In this context, consider the following samples from the writings of Locke, Rousseau, Smith and Mill, key prophets of Western liberal democracy:

If man in the state of nature be so free, as has been said: if he be absolute lord of his own person and possessions, equal to the greatest, and subject to no body, why will he part with his freedom? Why will he give up his empire, and subject himself to the dominion and control of any other power? To which it is obvious to answer, that though in the state of nature he hath such a right, yet enjoyment of it is very uncertain, and constantly exposed to the invasion of others: for all being kings as much as he, every man his equal, and the greater part no strict observers of equity and justice, the enjoyment of the property he has in this state is very unsafe, very unsecure. This makes him willing to quit a condition, which, however free, is full of fears and continual dangers: and it is not without reason, that he seeks out, and is willing to join in society with others, who are already united, or have a mind to unite, for the mutual preservation of their lives, liberties and estates, which I call by the general name, property. (Locke, Book II, Chapter IX, section 123)

... as a result of the contract they find themselves in a situation preferable in real terms to what prevailed before; instead of an alienation, they have profitably exchanged an uncertain and precarious life for a better and more secure one; they have exchanged natural independence for freedom, the power to injure others for the enjoyment of their own security; they have exchanged their own strength which others might overcome for a right which the social union makes invincible. (Rousseau, Book II, Chapter 4)

... the moment a people adopts representatives it is no longer free; it (freedom) no longer exists. (Rousseau, Book III, Chapter 15)

... the right of any individual over his own estate is always subordinate to the right of the community over everything; for without this there would be neither strength in the social bond nor effective force in the exercise of sovereignty. (Rousseau, Book I, Chapter 9)

Civil government supposes a certain subordination. (Smith, Book V, Chapter I, Part II)

The maxims are, first, that the individual is not accountable to society for his actions in so far as these concern the interests of no person but himself ... Secondly, that for such actions as are prejudicial to the interests of others, the individual is accountable and may be subjected either to social or to legal punishment if society is of the opinion that the one or the other is requisite for its protection. (Mill, Chapter V)

However, this idea of a submission to a higher omnipotent power, of surrender or sacrifice of freedom in favour of peace, prosperity and longevity, is not a new idea. It seems as old as recorded thought, and a consistent theme through the ages. Consider these examples:

No god indeed, not mortal, is beyond the might of thee, the mightyone; with the Maruts come hither, O Agni! (Rig-Veda, Book I, Hymn 19)

Concealed in the heart of all beings is the Atman, the Spirit, the Self; smaller than the smallest atom, greater than the vast spaces. The man who surrenders his human will leaves sorrows behind, and beholds the glory of the Atman by the grace of the Creator. (Upanishads, Katha Upanishad, Part 2)

You are the Father of the moving and unmoving world (animate and inanimate). You are the Guru worthy of worship, and of incomparable power. There is nobody equal to You. How could there be anybody greater than You in the three worlds? Therefore, bowing down and prostrating my body before you, O Supreme Lord, I seek to please you in order that You show tolerance to me like a father to his son, friend to friend, and lover to the beloved. (Gita, 11.43 and 11.44)

He who does his work for Me; he who considers Me as Supreme; he who is My devotee, free from attachment; he how has no enmity to all creatures; he comes (attains) to Me. O Pandava. (Gita, 11.55)

Surrender unto Him with all your being, O Bharata; by His grace, your will attain the Supreme peace and eternal abode. (Gita, 18.62)

Now then, if you will obey Me faithfully and keep My covenant, you shall be my treasured possession among all the peoples. Indeed, all the earth is Mine, but you shall be to me a Kingdom of priests and a holy nation. (Torah, Exodus, Chapter 19, verses 5 and 6).

My rules alone shall you observe, and faithfully follow my Laws: I the Lord am your God. (Torah, Leviticus, Chapter 18, verse 4)

My sheep hear my voice, and I know them, and they follow me; And I give them eternal life; and they shall never perish, neither shall any man pluck them out of my hand. My Father, which gave them me, is greater than all; and no man is able to pluck them out of my Father's hand. (Gospels, St. John, Chapter 10, verses 27 to 30)

He that hath my commandments, and keepeth them, he it is that loveth me; and he that loveth me shall be loved of my Father, and I will love him, will manifest myself to him. (Gospels, St. John, Chapter 14, verse 21)

Who but a foolish man would renounce the faith of Abraham? We chose him in this world, and in the world to come he shall abide among the righteous. When his Lord said to him: 'Submit,' he answered: 'I have submitted to the Lord of the Universe.' Abraham enjoined the faith on his children, and so did Jacob, saying: 'My children, God has chosen for you the true faith. Do not depart this except in full submissions.' (Koran, The Cow, 2:31-32)

Your God is one God; to Him surrender yourselves. Give good news to the humble, whose hearts are filled with awe at the mention of God; who endure adversity with fortitude, attend to their prayers, and give alms from what We gave them. (Koran, Pilgrimage, 22:33)

Those who submit to God and accept the true Faith; who are devout, sincere, patient, humble, charitable, and chaste; who fast and are mindful of God – on these, both men and women, God will bestow forgiveness and a rich recompense. (Koran, The Confederate Tribes, 33:35)

Filial piety and brotherly obedience are perhaps the roots of humanity, are they not? (Confucius, verse 1.2)

In terms of Rodney King's question, we must be cautious, judicious and precise in our use of "freedom" rhetoric. Everyone values freedom, but everyone has things they value even more. None of us who belongs to a society is truly free. We all recognize that our freedoms are not absolute. We give up significant natural freedom to attain other things we value more than freedom itself.

We should not use "freedom" to divide us, but should consider it as a marker in a hierarchy of values and use that marker to identify areas of commonality and disagreement.

There are things we put above the marker in order to live peacefully in our societies – like submitting to the rule of law, paying taxes and driving on the proper side of the road.

And there are things we put below the marker that we are prepared to protest, go to jail over or even die for in the name of defending our way of life – like submission to a foreign government, expropriation without compensation, universal suffrage or inequitable distribution of wealth and power.

It is fair to say everyone values freedom, but we may often have different beliefs in what other values rank above or below the freedom marker in our hierarchy of values. Accepting that we all both love and sacrifice freedom, and then defining and debating those individual values we put above and below the freedom marker, are steps to avoiding conflict and getting along.

Wealth: The Second Sacrifice

Of all the themes proposed in this book the most universal among these prophets concerns wealth and its accumulation. These prophets collectively issue a strong warning against the corrupting influence of wealth and material success and point out how misguided it is to make materialism a defining part of one's life. Their writing also contains a corresponding commandment to charity.

These prophets collectively acknowledge the inherent unfairness of wealth distribution in and between societies, and the lack of meaningful co-relation between material well-being and merit. In the older agricultural world this may have been based on observing of how the forces of nature have more to say about success than anything else, whether it is in weather conditions, climate changes, or the health and fecundity of crops, livestock or farmers.

In a more industrialized world the accidents of birth, upbringing or circumstances have a lot to say about how successful a person will be in the material world. Even in business the formula for success seems to include healthy portions of both luck and larceny.

Rare indeed is the wealthy person who can say that their wealth, or the poverty of others, is truly deserved; and surely only the most arrogant would argue that wealth and poverty are universally meted out based on the merit of their recipients.

In these matters, the prophets call for the sacrifice of wealth as a significant part of what it takes to get along in a fair and peaceful society. The examples are numerous and pervasive:

The two paths lie in front of man. Pondering on them, the wise man chooses the path of joy; the fool takes the path of pleasure. You have pondered, Nachiketas, on pleasures and you have rejected them. You have not accepted the chain of possessions wherewith men bind themselves beneath which they sink. (Upanishads, Katha Upanishad, Part 2)

To be bound by things of this world: this is bondage. To be free of them: this is liberation. (Upanishads, Maitri Upanishad, from 6.24)

The lovers of Brahmen seek him through the sacred Vedas, through holy sacrifices, charity, penance and abstinence. (Upanishads, The Supreme Teaching, Liberation)

The wise ones, established in intuitive intelligence, certainly give up fruits of their actions, are liberated from the bondage of birth and death, and reach salubrious (Anâmayam) supreme bliss. (Gita, 2.51)

Sacrifices are made in the form of material possession, austerities, yogic practices, Vedic studies, intuitive wisdom, and severe vows as by disciplined persons. (Gita, 4.28)

Charity given to the deserving, who can make no return, in a proper place and time and to a worthy person, is regarded as sattvic. (Gita, 17.20)

And how is a family man accomplished in generosity? Here, Byagghapajja, a family man dwells at home with a mind devoid of the stain of stinginess, freely generous, open-handed, delighting in relinquishment, one devoted to charity, delighting in giving and sharing. In this was a family man is accomplished in generosity. (Canon, page 126)

O monks, if people knew, as I know, the result of giving and sharing, they would not eat without having given, nor would they allow the stain of niggardliness to obsess them and take root in their minds. Even if it were their last morsel, their last mouthful, they would not eat without having shared it, if there was someone to share it with. But, monks, people do not know, as I know, the result of giving and sharing, they eat without having given, and the stain of niggardliness obsesses them and takes root in their minds. (Canon, page 169)

When you reap the harvest of your land, you shall not reap all the way to the edges of your field, or gather the gleanings of your harvest. You shall not pick your vineyard bare, or gather the fallen fruit of your vineyard; you shall leave them for the poor and the stranger: I the Lord am your God. (Torah, Leviticus, verses 9–10)

Lay not up for yourselves treasures upon earth, where moth and rust doth corrupt, and where thieves break through and steal; But lay up for yourselves treasures in heaven, where neither moth nor rust doth corrupt, and where thieves do not break through nor steal; For where your treasure is, there will be your heart also. (Gospels, St. Matthew, Chapter 6, verses 19-21).

Then said he also to him that bade him, When thou makest a dinner or supper, call not thy friends, nor thy brethren, neither thy kinsmen nor thy rich neighbours; lest they also bid thee again, and a recompence be made thee. But when thou makest a feast, call the poor, the maimed, the lame, the blind: And thou shalt be blessed; for they cannot recompense thee: for thou shalt be recompensed at the resurrection of the just. (Gospels, St. Luke, Chapter 14, verses 12-14)

Now when Jesus heard this things, he said unto him, Yet lackest thou one thing: sell all that thou hast, and distribute unto the poor, and thou shalt have treasure in heaven: and come, follow me. And when he heard this, he was very sorrowful: for he was very rich. And when Jesus saw that he was very sorrowful, he said, How hardly shall they that have riches enter into the kingdom of God! For it is easier for a camel to go through a needle's eye than for a rich man to enter into the kingdom of God. (Gospels, St. Luke, Chapter 18, verses 22-25)

The righteous man is he who believes in God and the Last Day, in the angels and the Book and the prophets; who, though he loves it dearly, gives away his wealth to kinsfolk, to orphans, to the destitute, to the traveller in need and to beggars, and for the redemption of captives; who attends to his prayers and renders the alms levy ... (Koran, The Cow, 2:176)

Be charitable; God loves the charitable. (Koran, The Cow, 2:195)

Have faith in God and His apostle and give in alms of that which He has made your inheritance; for whichever of you believes and gives in alms shall be richly recompensed. (Koran, Iron, 17:7)

Each person's every joint must perform a charity every day the sun comes up: ... (Forty Hadith, Hadith 26)

Duke Jing of Qi possessed a thousand teams of four horses each. On the day of his death, people found no virtue to praise him with. Bo-yi and Shu-qi starved at the foot of Mount Shou-yang. People to this day still praise them.

This is perhaps what it [the Way, humanity] means. (Confucius, 16:12)

The Master said: "When Chi departed for Qi, he rode a fat horse and wore a soft fur robe. I hear it: 'The gentleman relieves the hard-pressed; he does not add to the rich.'" (Confucius, 6:4)

Wealth and place breed insolence That brings ruin in its train. (Tao, Chapter 9)

He who has hoarded most will suffer the heaviest loss. Be content with what you have and are, and no one can despoil you; Who stops in time nothing can harm. He is forever safe and secure. (Tao, Chapter 44)

Heaven's way is like the bending of a bow. When a bow is bent the top comes down and the bottom-end comes up. So too does Heaven take away from those who have too much, and give it to those who have not enough. But if it is Heaven's way to take from those who have too much and give to those who have not enough, this is far from being man's way. He takes away from those that have not enough in order to make offering to those who already have too much. (Tao, Chapter 77)

The Sage has no need to hoard; When his own last scrap has been used up on behalf of others, Lo, he has more than before! When his own last scrap has been used up in giving to others, Lo, he has more than before! When his own last scrap has been used up in giving to others, Lo, his stock is even greater than before! For Heaven's way is to sharpen without cutting. And the Sage's way is to act without striving. (Tao, Chapter 81)

If the Gospel and the apostles may be credited, no man can be Christian without charity and without that faith which works, not by force, but by love. (Locke, Letter, page 150)

Under a bad government, this equality is only an appearance and an illusion; it serves only to keep the poor in their wretchedness and sustain the rich in their usurpation. In truth, laws are always useful to those with possessions and harmful to those who have nothing; from which it follows that the social state is advantageous to men only when all possess something and none too much. (Rousseau, Book I, Chapter 9, concluding footnote)

Do you want coherence in the state? Then bring the two extremes as close together as possible; have neither very rich men nor beggars, for these two estates, naturally inseparable, are equally fatal to the common good; from the one class comes friends of tyranny, from the other, tyrants. It is always these two classes which make commerce of the public freedom: the one buys, the other sells. (Rousseau, Book II, Chapter 11, footnote)

All for ourselves, and nothing for other people, seems in every age of the world, to have been the vile maxim of the masters of mankind. (Smith, Book II, Chapter IV)

When considering Rodney King's question, nothing is more important than considering disparities in wealth and quality of life. We need to look for economic differences that may be contributing to social, political and ideological differences and openly and honestly discuss and address them.

As the prophets have pointed out, one test will be of the rich, who will have to consider the extent and nature of the sacrifices they need and should make in order to get along. Another test will be of the poor, who will have to consider what they can and should do to be that part of Lao Tzu's bow which bends upward. In this respect, the co-relation between education and opportunity is unmistakable in our modern world, and when it comes to education there is a possible partnership between rich and poor.

The rich can take responsibility for funding education, and the poor can take responsibility for taking advantage of the opportunity education represents. In the end, they both should win.

Violence: The Third Sacrifice

The final sacrifice most often referred to by these prophets is the sacrifice of violence. What we call chaos, disorder or disaster is often the natural use of violence by those most capable of wielding it. Humanity generally abhors it.

We also recognize that most of us have the capability of extreme violence within us, both individually and culturally. Even the most modest review of the history of human conflict confirms the atrocities any kind of society can talk itself into committing under the umbrella of revenge, defense of self or others, first strike, or entitlement.

What these prophets require is that we sacrifice our ability and entitlement to individual violence, and surrender violence to society as a whole as represented by our communities and the governments they choose. While not a topic considered by all the prophets reviewed in this book, the condemnation of violence and the plea for peace crosses all major ideological movements considered, both religious and political. Here are some examples:

... for where-ever violence is used, and injury done, though by hands appointed to administer justice, it is still violence and injury, however coloured with the name, pretences, or

forms of the law, the end of whereof being to protect and redress the innocent, by an unbiased application of it, to all who are under it ... (Locke, Two Treatises, Book II, Chapter III)

To avoid this state of war ... is one great reason of men's putting themselves into society, and quitting the state of nature: for where there is an authority, a power on earth, from which relief can be had by appeal, there the continuance of the state of war is excluded, and the controversy is decided by that power. (Locke, Two Treatises, Book II, Chapter III)

... as a result of the contract they find themselves in a situation preferable in real terms to what prevailed before; instead of an alienation, they have profitably exchanged an uncertain and precarious life for a better and more secure one; they have exchanged natural independence for freedom, the power to injure others for the enjoyment of their own security; they have exchanged their own strength which others might overcome for a right which the social union makes invincible. (Rousseau, Book II, Chapter 4)

Ji Kang-zi asked Master Kong about government, saying: "If I kill those who have lost the Way to move closer to those who possess the Way – what do you think of it?" Master Kong replied: "Sir, in conducting government, why must you resort to killing? If you desire goodness, the people will be good accordingly. The gentleman's moral character is wind and the small man's moral character, grass. When the grass is visited by the wind, it must surely bend." (Confucius, 12.19)

He who by Tao purposes to help a ruler of men Will oppose all conquest by force of arms; For such things are wont to rebound. Where armies are, thorns and brambles grow. The raising of a great host is followed by a year of dearth.

Therefore a good general effects his purpose and then stops; he does not take further advantage to victory. Fulfills his purpose and does not glory in what he has done; Fulfills his purpose and does not boast of what he has done; Fulfills his purpose, but takes no pride in what he has done; Fulfills his purpose, but only as a step that could not be avoided. Fulfills his purpose, but without violence; For what has a time of vigour also has a time of decay. This is against Tao, And what is against Tao will soon perish. (Tao, Chapter 30)

Fight of the sake of God those that fight against you, but do not attack them first. God does not love aggressors. (Koran, The Cow, 2:190)

Do not make God, when you swear by Him, a means to prevent you from dealing justly, from guarding yourselves against evil, and from making peace among men. (Koran, The Cow, 2:224)

If they incline to make peace with you, make peace with them, and put your trust in God. It is surely He who hears all and knows all. (Koran, The Spoils, 8:60)

It may well be that God will put good will between you and those with whom you have hitherto been at odds. God is mighty, God is forgiving and merciful. God does not forbid you to be kind and equitable to those who have neither made war on your religion nor driven you from your homes. God loves the equitable. (Koran, She Who Is Tested, 60:7)

Blessed are the meek: for they shall inherit the earth ... Blessed are the merciful: for they shall obtain mercy ... Blessed are the peacemakers: for they shall be called the children of God. (Gospels, St. Matthew, Chapter 5, verses 5, 7 and 9)

And the soldiers likewise demanded of him, saying, And what shall we do? And he said unto them, Do violence to no man ... (Gospels, St. Luke, Chapter 3, verse 14)

Sri Bhagavan said: Fearlessness, purity of mind, steadiness in yoga of knowledge, charity, self-control, sacrifice, study of scriptures, austerity, rectitude, Ahimsa [non-violence] truthfulness, freedom from anger, renunciation, tranquility, abstaining from slander, compassion to all creatures, absence of greed, gentleness, modesty, absence of fickleness (absence of agitation), vigor, forgiveness, fortitude, cleanliness, absence of malice, and absence of pride; These are the qualities of the one born of divine nature, O Bharata. (Gita, 16.1-16.3)

Here, monks, a noble disciple gives up the destruction of life and abstains from it. By abstaining from the destruction of life, the noble disciple gives to immeasurable beings freedom from fear, hostility, and oppression. By giving immeasurable beings freedom from fear, hostility and oppression, he himself will enjoy immeasurable freedom from fear, hostility, and oppression. This is the first of the great gifts and the fourth stream of merit. (Canon, page 173)

In the context of what we have to do to get along, and in answer to Rodney King's question, the prophets' advice is that violence matters. This is more important today than in any previous time in human history, as military technology makes weapons of mass destruction out of our planet's smallest creatures and nature's most basic forces.

Firearms of any conceivable type are available to anyone with the money and willpower to have them. If we are going to get along in the modern world we need to heed the prophets' message, not just individually but as families, communities and nations, and sacrifice our natural right to commit violence in favour of institutions which can peacefully and fairly resolve our disputes. We must collectively agree there will never be security *for* us until there is security *from* us, and that the only way to truly ensure security for some is to ensure security for all.

A Common Collective Wisdom

These chapters can only contain samples of the many verses and pages devoted by these prophets to the idea of sacrifice, especially the sacrifices of freedom, wealth and violence.

However, what matters most is the extent to which there is collective agreement around the need for these sacrifices to get along; a collective agreement that crosses time, geography, inspiration and ideology.

In our modern world, these sacrifices really matter. We must look to the choices we make, as individuals, communities and nations, and ask ourselves if we are prepared to recognize the need for these sacrifices in order to get along in a modern and civilized world.

We must also look to those of us that are not willing to make these sacrifices and openly challenge their failure to do so as the most significant contribution to ongoing conflict between and among people.

In doing so, however, we must not let self-righteousness become the basis of hypocrisy. In that regard, these prophets suggest some very important values that buttress and support these three key sacrifices. Those values are the subject of the next chapter.

4 Six Values

As well as teaching that sacrifice matters, these prophets teach that values matter too. Some principles are more important to us than others. By identifying, understanding and consistently applying those principles we can lead happier and more fulfilling lives.

However, values are subjective, both personally and culturally; and values may and do conflict. Our most difficult decisions are made when two or more principles we hold important suggest opposite or conflicting behaviours.

The choices we make in these circumstances reveal which of these principles is most important to us in that situation, and therefore what we value most.

Over time, all the choices we make add up to a clear picture of what is most important to us, despite what we might we think our values are.

Since our values determine and guide our behaviour they are absolutely critical in considering Rodney King's question and why we can or cannot get along.

If there is a common worldview to be discovered or developed, defining our common values is the meeting place where such a discovery can be made.

In the previous chapter I identified three sacrifices collectively supported by our common prophets – freedom, charity and non-violence. In this chapter I identity six values these prophets suggest are of critical importance in getting along – tolerance, self-reflection, humility, compassion, inclusiveness and reciprocity.

In each case there is a remarkable degree of support and consensus among these prophets that spans their historical, geographic, political and philosophical differences.

In considering these values in the context of getting long, bear in mind that their strength is in their collective.

While each of these values by themselves can be a significant contributor to our getting along with each other, their real significance comes in their collective implementation.

Tolerance: The First Value

Foremost among these values, and of critical importance to Rodney King's question, is tolerance.

Throughout civilization our great philosophers have promoted tolerance as a founding principle for fairness, humanity and peaceful co-existence.

To illustrate this principle, I begin with examples from the Qur'an. It is not just recent events that lead me to begin my examples here. Mohammad preaches tolerance as much as any other prophet considered here, and more often than most. Here are some examples:

As for those that serve other masters besides Him, God Himself is watching them. You are not accountable for what they do. (Koran, Counsel, 42.5)

Bear patiently with what they [the unbelievers] say, and leave their company without recrimination. Leave to Me those that deny the Truth ... (Koran, The Mantled One, 73:12)

If it was God's will to punish men for their misdeeds, not one creature would be left alive on the earth's surface. He respites them till an appointed time. And when their time comes, they shall learn that God has been watching all His servants. (Koran, The Creator, 35:34)

Therefore give warning. Your duty is only to give warning: you are not their keeper. As for those that turn their backs and disbelieve, God will inflict on them the supreme chastisement. To Us they shall return, and We will bring them to account. (Koran, The Dawn, 88:20-88:26)

Say: 'Unbelievers, I do not worship what you worship, nor do you worship what I worship. I shall never worship what you worship, nor will you even worship what I worship. You have your own religion, and I have mine.' (Koran, The Unbelievers, 109.1:109.6)

Part of someone's being a good Muslim is his leaving alone that which does not concern him. (Forty Hadith, Hadith 12)

However, Mohammad is not unusual among the religious prophets for advocating tolerance. Consider these examples:

A learned humble Brahmin, a cow, an elephant, a dog, and even a dog-eater are seen with an equal eye be a punditah (sage). (Gita, 5.18)

He, who is tranquil in pain and pleasure, abides in his own self, regards that a clod, a stone and gold are equal; to whom the desireable and the undesireable are one and the same; who maintains composure in blame and praise; and who considers honor and dishonor equal; who regards friends and foes alike; and who abandons all (self-serving) initiatives, is said to transcend the Gunas. (Gita, 14.24-14.25)

"Monks, there are these five courses of speech that others may use when they address you: their speech may be timely or untimely, true or untrue, gentle or harsh, connected with good or with harm, spoken with a mind of loving-kindness or in a mood hate ... Herein, monks, you should train thus: 'Our minds will remain unaffected, and we shall utter no bitter words; we shall abide compassionate for their welfare, with a mind of loving-kindness, never in a mood of hate. We shall abide pervading that person with a mind imbued with loving-kindness, and starting with that person, we shall abide pervading the all-encompassing world with a mind imbued with loving-kindness, abundant, exalted, immeasurable, without hostility, and without ill-will.' That is how you should train, monks ..." (Canon, page 278)

Jesus said unto him, Thou shall love the Lord thy God with all thy heart, and with all they soul, and with all thy mind. This is the first great commandment. And the second is like unto it, Thou shalt love they neighbour as thyself. On these two commandments hang all the law and the prophets. (Gospels, St. Matthew, Chapter 22, verses 37-40)

These things I command you, that ye love one another. (Gospels, St. John, Chapter 15, verse 17)

Tolerance is also a major theme of the more political prophets considered in this book. Here are some examples:

Zi-gong asked: "Is there one single word that one can practice throughout one's life?" The Master said: "It is perhaps 'like-hearted considerateness' 'What you do not wish for yourself, do not impose on others.'" (Confucius, 15.24)

Those who of old won the adherence of all who live under heaven All did so by not interfering. Had they interfered, They would not have won this adherence. (Tao, Chapter 48)

But the adherence of all under heaven can only be won by letting-alone. (Tao, Chapter 57)

If any man err from the right way, it is his own misfortune, no injury to thee; nor therefore art thou to punish him in the things of this life because thou supposest he will be miserable in that which is to come. (Locke, Letter, page 156)

It is not enough that ecclesiastical men abstain from violence and rapine and all manner of persecution. He that pretends to be a successor of the apostles, and takes upon him the office of teaching, is obliged also to admonish his hearers of the duties of peace and goodwill towards all men, as well towards the erroneous as the orthodox; towards those that differ from them in faith and worship as well as towards those that agree with them therein. And he ought industriously to exhort all men, whether private persons or magistrates (if any such there be in his church), to charity, meekness and toleration, and diligently endeavour to ally and temper all that heat and unreasonable averseness of mind with either any man's fiery zeal for his own sect or craft of others has kindled against dissenters. (Locke, Letter, page 158)

It is not the diversity of opinions (which cannot be avoided), but the refusal of toleration to those that are of different opinions (which might have been granted), that has produced all the bustles and wars that have been in the

Christian world on account of religion. (Locke, Letter, page 175)

Now it is very important to the state that each citizen should have a religion which makes him love his duty, but the dogmas of that religion are of interest neither to the state nor its members, except in so far as those dogmas concern morals and the duties which everyone who professes that religion is bound to perform towards others. Moreover, everyone may hold whatever opinion he pleases, without the sovereign having any business to take cognizance of them. For the sovereign has no competence in the other world; whatever may be the fate of the subjects in the life to come, it is nothing to do with the sovereign, so long as they are good citizens in life. (Rousseau, Contract, Book IV, Chapter 8)

As for the negative dogmas, I would limit them to a single one: no intolerance. Intolerance is something which belongs to the religions we have rejected. (Rousseau, Contract, Book IV, Chapter 8)

Wherever theological intolerance is admitted, it is bound to have some civil consequences, and when it does so, the sovereign is no longer sovereign, even in the temporal sphere; at this stage the priests become the real masters, and kings are only their officers. Not that there is not, and can no longer be, an exclusive national religion, all religions which themselves tolerate others must be tolerated, provided only that their dogmas contain nothing contrary to the duties of the citizen. (Rousseau, Contract, Book IV, Chapter 8)

In a country where the law favoured the teachers of no one religion more than those of another, it would not be necessary that any of them should have any particular or immediate dependency upon the sovereign or executive power; or that he should have any thing to do, either in appointing, or in dismissing them from their offices. In such a situation he would have no occasion to give himself any concern about them, further than to keep the peace among them, in the same manner as among the rest of his subjects; that is, to hinder them from persecuting, abusing, or oppressing one another. (Smith, Wealth, Book V, Chapter I, Part III)

But the peculiar evil of silencing the expression of an opinion is that it is robbing the human race, posterity as well as the existing generation – those who dissent from the opinion, still more than those who hold it. If the opinion is right, they are deprived of the opportunity of exchanging error for truth; if it wrong, they lose, what is almost as great a benefit, the clearer perception and livelier impression of truth produced by its collision with error. (Mill, Liberty, Chapter II)

Truth, in the great practical concerns of life, is so much a question of the reconciling and combining of opposites that very few have minds sufficiently capacious and impartial to make the adjustment with an approach to correctness, and it has to be made by the rough process of a struggle between combatants fighting under hostile banners ... I am aware that there is not, in this country, any intolerance of differences of opinion on most of these topics. They are adduced to show, by admitted and multiplied examples, the universality of the fact that only through diversity of opinion is there, in the existing state of human intellect, a chance of fair play to all sides of the truth. When there are persons to be found who form an exception to the apparent unanimity of the world on any subject, even if the world is in the right, it is always probable that dissentients have something worth hearing to say for themselves, and that truth would lose something by their silence. (Mill, Liberty, Chapter II)

It remains to be proved that society or any of its officers holds a commission from on high to avenge any supposed offence to Omnipotence which is not also a wrong to our fellow creatures ... It is a determination not to tolerate others in doing what is permitted by their religion, because it is not permitted by the persecutor's religion. It is a belief that God not only abominates the act of the misbeliever, but will not hold us guiltless if we leave him unmolested. (Mill, Liberty, Chapter IV)

In terms of getting along, tolerance is a basic value to live by. How much better could the world be if we were all as tolerant of others as we want others to be of us?

Tolerance, however, does not have to mean submission. As Rousseau points out, tolerance is a two way street. There can be limits to tolerance, especially tolerance of and for the intolerant. Human nature is such that tolerance without reciprocity can be a greater source of conflict than the condition that was tolerated to begin with.

Self-Reflection: The Second Value

The tolerance advocated by these prophets results perhaps from their strong belief in honest self-reflection as an important value and activity, as well as a belief among many of these prophets that the source of spiritual happiness and contentment is something within each of us and is not something to be found in an outer world.

Tolerance should not be hard to develop if we take an honest look at ourselves, as none of us is perfect as we might sometimes think we are. If we take some time to enquire we should find we are as much in need of tolerance from others as they are in need of tolerance from us.

Self-reflection is also another significant value that helps us deal with Rodney King's question. We need to have as frank an assessment of ourselves as we do of others, not only if we are going to be fair in how we see, treat and deal with others but also if we are going to fairly defend or advocate for ourselves when it comes to how they see, treat and deal with us.

There can be no greater source of heartache in human relations than to misperceive what we portray to others, or to have our self-assurance exceed our self-awareness. Consider these examples from the prophets considered in this book:

Only those who see God in their soul attain the joy eternal. (Upanishads, Svetasvatara Upanishad, Part 6)

Even as fire without finds peace in its resting-place, when thoughts become silence the soul finds peace in its own source. And when a mind which longs for truth finds the peace of its own source, then those false inclinations cease which were the result of former actions done in the delusion of the senses. Samsara, the transmigration of life, takes place in one's own mind. Let one therefore keep the mind pure, for what a man thinks that he becomes: this is a mystery of Eternity. (Upanishads, Maitri Upanishad)

He, who finds happiness, pleasure and the inner light within his self, is a yogin and attains Brahman and the bliss of Brahman or beatitude of Brahmin. (Gita, 5.24)

He should pull (lift) himself up by his own self and not let himself sink, for the Self is the friend of the self and also the Self can be the enemy of the self. (Gita, 6.5)

And what, monks, is right mindfulness? Here, monks, a monk dwells contemplating the body in the body, ardent, clearly comprehending, mindful, having removed longing and dejection in regard to the world. He dwells contemplating feelings in feelings, ardent, clearly comprehending, mindful, having removed longing and dejection in regard to the world. He dwells contemplating mind in mind, ardent, clearly comprehending, mindful, having removed longing and dejection in regard to the world. He dwells contemplating phenomena in phenomena, ardent, clearly comprehending, mindful, having removed longing and dejection in regard to the world. This is called right mindfulness. (Canon, page 240)

Any why beholdest thou the mote that is in thy brother's eye, but perceivest not the beam that is in thine own eye? Either how canst thou say to thy brother, Brother, let me pull out the mote that is in thine eye, when thou thyself beholdest not the beam that is in thine own eye? (Gospels, St. Luke, Chapter 6, verses 41-42)

For from within, out of the heart of men, proceed evil thoughts, adulteries, fornications, murders, Thefts, covetnous, wickedness, deceit, lasciviousness, and evil eye, blasphemy, pride, foolishness; All these evil things come from within, and defile the man. (Gospels, St. Mark, Chapter 7, verses 21-23)

And the scribes and Pharisees brought unto him a woman taken in adultery; and when they had set her in the midst, They said unto him, Master, this woman was taken in adultery, in the very act. Now Moses in the law commanded us, that such should be stoned: but what sayest thou? This they said, tempting him, that they might accuse him. But Jesus stooped down, and with his finger wrote on the ground, as though he had heard them not. So when they continued asking him, he lifted himself, and said unto them, He that is without sin among you, let him first caste a stone at her. And again he stooped down, and wrote on the ground. And they which heard it, being convicted by their own conscience, went out one by one, beginning at the eldest, even unto the last: and Jesus was left alone, and the woman standing in the midst. When Jesus lifted up himself, and saw none but the woman, he said unto her, Woman, where are those thine accusers? hath no man condemned thee? She said, No man, Lord. And Jesus said unto her, Neither do I condemn thee: go and sin no more. (Gospels,, St. John, Chapter 8, verses 3-11)

Whatever good befalls you, it is from God; and whatever ill from yourself. (Koran, Women, 4:82)

God does not change a people's lot unless they change what is in their hearts. (Koran, Thunder, 13:11)

Truly in the body there is a morsel of flesh which, if it be whole, all the body is whole and which, if it be diseased, all of it is diseased. Truly it is the heart. (Forty Hadith, Hadith 6)

Everyone starts his day and is a vendor of his soul, either freeing it or bringing about its ruin. (Forty Hadith, Hadith 23)

Master Zeng said: "I daily thrice examine myself. In counseling men, have I not been wholeheartedly sincere? In associating with friends, have I not been truthful to my word? In transmitting something, have I not been proficient?" (Confucius, 1.4)

The Master said: "On seeing a worthy man, think of equaling him; on seeing an unworthy man, examine yourself inwardly." (Confucius, 4.17)

The Master said: "Virtue uncultivated, learning undiscussed, the inability to move toward righteousness after hearing it, and the inability to correct my imperfections – these are my anxieties." (Confucius, 7.3)

The Master said: "Be more demanding with yourself and less so with others and you shall keep resentment away." (Confucius, 15.15)

The Master said: "The gentleman seeks it [the Way] in himself; the small man seeks it in others." (Confucius, 15.20)

It [the Tao] is there within us all the while; Draw upon it as you will, it never runs dry. (Tao, Chapter 6)

Whosoever will list himself under the banner of Christ, must, in the first place and above all things, make war upon his own lusts and vices. It is in vain for any man to usurp the name of Christian, without holiness of life, purity of manners, benignity and meekness of spirit. (Locke, Letter, page 150)

If the cultivation of the understanding consists in one thing more than in another, it is surely in learning the grounds of one's own opinions. (Mill, Chapter II)

Humility: The Third Value

Humility is another value for getting along advocated by the prophets considered in this book. Humility is a natural result of the honest self-reflection they also ask of us.

After all, an honest self-assessment of our strengths and weaknesses can only be a humbling experience, whether we do it as individuals, communities or countries.

There are always areas where others outperform us, or we can do better, or we are not living up to our own expectations or beliefs.

The promotion of humility as a value is advocated by these prophets across time, geography and philosophical tradition. Consider these examples:

Whenever the soul has thoughts of "I" and "mine" it binds itself with its lower self, as a bird with the net of a snare. (Upanishads, Maitri Upanishad)

Humility, non-ostentation (Adambhitvam), non-violence, patience, straightforwardness, service to an Âcârya, purity, steadfastness, self-restraint, aversion toward sense objects, absence of egoism ... are declared the knowledge, and that which is otherwise is non-knowledge. (Gita, 13.7-13.9)

This is the way, student, that leads to a low birth, namely, one is obstinate and arrogant ... and does not honor, respect, revere, and venerate one who should be honored, respected, revered, and venerated. (Canon, page 164)

People for the most part delight in conceit, take delight in conceit, rejoice in conceit. But when the Dhamma is taught by the Tathāgata for the abolition of conceit, people wish to listen to it, lend an ear, and try to understand it. (Canon, page 191)

At the same time came the disciples unto Jesus, saying, Who is the greatest in the kingdom of heaven? And Jesus called a little child unto him, and set him in the midst of them, And said, Verily I say unto you, Except ye be converted, and become as little children, ye shall not enter into the kingdom of heaven. Whosoever therefore shall humble himself as this little child, the same is greatest in the kingdom of heaven. (Gospels, St. Matthew, Chapter 18, verses 1-4)

Two men went up into the temple to pray; the one a Pharisee, and the other a publican. The Pharisee stood and prayed thus with himself, God, I thank thee, that I am not as other men are, extortioners, unjust, adulterers, or even this publican. I fast twice in the week, I give tithes of all that I possess. And the publican, standing afar off, would not lift up as much as his eyes unto heaven, but smote upon his breast, saying, God be merciful to me a sinner. I tell you, this man went down to his house justified rather than the other: for everyone that exalteth himself shall be abased; and he that humbleth himself shall be exalted. (Gospels, St. Luke, Chapter 18, verses 10-14)

As for those that have faith and do good works, God will bestow on them their rewards and enrich them from His own abundance. But those who are scornful and proud He will sternly punish, and they will find none besides God to protect or help them. (Koran, Women, 4:173)

Do not walk proudly on earth. You cannot split the earth, nor can you rival the mountains in stature. (Koran, The Night Journey, 17:37)

True servants of the Merciful are those who walk humbly on the earth ... (Koran, Al-Furqān, 25:62)

Do not treat men with scorn, nor walk proudly on the earth: God does not love the arrogant and vainglorious. Rather, let your stride be modest and your voice low: the most hideous of voices is the braying of the ass. (Koran, Luqmān, 31:18)

The Master said: "... A distinguished man is one who is upright in substance and loves righteousness, who examines people's words and observes their facial expressions, and who is anxious to remain humble to others. Such a man is always distinguished in a state and always distinguished in a noble house." (Confucius, 12.20)

Zi-gong asked: "What must a man be like to be called shi?" The Master said: "In conducting himself, he has a sense of shame; ... (Confucius, 13.20)

The Master said: "The gentleman is self-possessed and not swaggering; the small man is swaggering and not self-possessed." (Confucius, 13.26)

Therefore the Sage Puts himself in the background; but is always to the fore. Remains outside; but is always there. Is it not just because he does not strive for any personal end That all his personal ends are fulfilled? (Tao, Chapter 7)

So too the Sage just because he never at any time makes a show of greatness in fact achieves greatness. (Tao, Chapter 34)

Therefore the Sage knows himself but does not show himself. Knows his own value, but does not put himself on high. (Tao, Chapter 72)

And for the very reason that he does not call attention to what he does He is not ejected from fruition of what he has done. (Tao, Chapter 2)

Let anyone have never so true a claim to all these things, yet if he be destitute of charity, meekness, and good-will in general towards all mankind, even to those that are not Christians, he is certainly yet short of being a true Christian himself. (Locke, Letter, page 150)

In terms of Rodney King's question, humility makes it easier to get along with others. It is a "no-lose" value. If we truly deserve to be humble, then we will have avoided provoking the sort of reaction from others that can lead to ridicule, scorn or conflict.

On other hand, if we are sincerely modest when we have something to brag about, our humility can only increase our merit. A common paradox is that those who find it hardest to be humble often have the least to brag about. If we have trouble being humble, as individuals, communities or nations then we should be on guard against ourselves.

Compassion: The Fourth Value

A further value emphasized in the teachings of these prophets is compassion, a value with profound possibilities in terms of Rodney King's question. After all, what could be more helpful in terms of getting along than to feel and acknowledge each other's suffering and perhaps even want to do something about it?

Compassion connects our emotions and our intellect. It requires us to investigate, understand and appreciate as well as feel.

True compassion requires us to understand the causes of suffering as well as the mere fact that suffering exists.

In this respect compassion is more than empathy. Empathy only requires us to feel the suffering of others. Compassion requires us to feel that suffering but also to appreciate its causes. For these reasons compassion can be a powerful force for avoiding or resolving conflict.

Here are some extracts from the teachings of these prophets in support of compassion:

Out of compassion (anukampâ-artham), I destroy their (Ajnâna and Tamashah) ignorance and darkness by abiding in their self (Âmabhâvasthah) with the light of wisdom (shining lamp of wisdom). (Gita, 10.11)

He who has no hatred of all living beings, friendly, compassionate, free from I-ness and free from ego; is same in pleasure and pain, and patient; Yogi who is ever self-content, self-controlled, determined in his faith in Me, with his mind and intelligence dwelling upon me (he is My devotee), is dear to Me. (Gita, 12.13-12.14)

Here, monks, some person dwells pervading one-quarter with a mind imbued with compassion, likewise the second quarter, the third, and the fourth. Thus above, below, across, and everywhere, and to all as to himself, he dwells pervading the entire world with a mind imbued with compassion, vast, exalted, measureless, without hostility, without ill will. He relishes it, takes a liking to it, and is thrilled by it. (Canon, page 216)

'Our minds will remain unaffected, and we shall utter no bitter words; we shall abide compassionate for their welfare, with a mind of loving-kindness, never in a mood of hate. We shall abide pervading that person with a mind imbued with loving-kindness, and starting with that person, we shall abide pervading the all-encompassing world with a mind imbued with loving-kindness, abundant, exalted, immeasurable, without hostility, and without ill-will.' (Canon, page 278)

But he, willing to justify himself, said unto Jesus, And who is my neighbour? And Jesus answering said, A certain man went down to from Jerusalem to Jericho, and fell among thieves, which stripped him of his raiment, and wounded him, and departed, leaving him half dead. And by chance there came down a certain priest that way: and when he saw him, he passed by on the other side. And likewise a Levite, when he was at the place, came and looked on him, and passed by on the other side. But a certain Samaritan, as he journeyed, came where he was; and when he saw him, he had compassion on him, And went to him and bound up his wounds, pouring oil and wine, and set him on his own beast, and brought him to an inn, and took care of him. And on the morrow when he departed, he took out two pence, and gave them to the host, and said unto him, Take care of him; and whatsoever thou spendest more, when I come again, I will repay thee. Which now of these three, thinkest thou, was neighbour unto him that fell among the thieves? And he said, He that shewed mercy on him. Then said Jesus unto him, Go and do thou likewise. (Gospels, St. Luke, Chapter 10, verses 29-37)

Praise be to God, Lord of the Universe, The Compassionate, the Merciful, Sovereign of the Day of Judgment! (Koran, The Exordium)

The day will surely come when each soul will be confronted with whatever good it did. As for its evil deeds, it will wish they were a long way off. God admonishes you to fear Him. God is compassionate towards His servants. Say: 'If you love God, follow me. God will love you and forgive you your sins. God is forgiving and merciful.' (Koran, The 'Imrans, 3:30)

Your God is one God. There is no god but Him. He is the Compassionate, the Merciful. (Koran, The Cow, 2:163)

The Master said: "'If benevolent men were to rule a state a hundred years, they would be able to tame brutes and abolish capital punishment' How true this saying rings!" (Confucius, 13.11)

The Master said: "People need humanity more than water and fire. As for water and fire, I have seen people tread them and die, but I have never seen anyone die from treading humanity." (Confucius, 15.35)

Therefore the Sage Is all the time in the most perfect way helping men, He certainly does not turn his back on men; Is all the time in the most perfect way helping creatures, He certainly does not turn his back on creatures. (Tao, Chapter 27)

Here are my three treasures. Guard and keep them! The first is pity ... Heaven arms with pity those whom it would not see destroyed. (Tao, Chapter 67)

... for the end of government being the preservation of all, as much as may be, even the guilty are to be spared, where it can prove no prejudice to the innocent. (Locke, Two Treatises, Book II, Chapter XIV)

If the Gospel and the apostles may be credited, no man can be a Christian without charity and without that faith which works, not by force, but by love. (Locke, Letter, page 150)

Inclusiveness: The Fifth Value

Even those that cultivate compassion can run afoul of a selective spirit. One way to avoid the risk of selective cruelty or hypocrisy is to maintain and draw upon a deep well of compassion for all humankind.

This principle leads to inclusiveness, another value proposed by the prophets considered in this book. Their inclusive approach to humanity is repeated throughout almost all the teachings considered here.

Inclusiveness helps reduce conflict. It requires us to consider others as part of our group. We tend to treat insiders with more patience, tolerance and forgiveness than we treat outsiders, whether the insiders are family, members of the same faith or community, or even members of the same nation.

The way we handle conflict within our group can be quite different than how we deal with conflict between groups or between ourselves and others outside our group. If both sides to a conflict can see themselves as being members of the same group, then they are more likely to find a way to avoid conflict, or resolve developing conflicts with less intensity. In this way, inclusiveness helps avoid conflict.

The absence of inclusiveness, on the other hand, is exclusivity. Exclusivity puts us on the inside and others on the outside. It can go a long way toward explaining why we may be having trouble getting along. Exclusivity provokes criticism and resentment from those not in our group, and arrogance and inhumanity from those who are.

There is consensus among these prophets that one goal of a society, religion or philosophy is to find peace and security for humankind as a whole, not just for the most direct adherents or believers.

They also suggest this can be done *without* unanimity on all things. Their formula for peace and security includes an inclusive world-view that embraces a concern and compassion for all humanity and places each of us, as individuals, families, communities and nations, within the larger and all-encompassing human family.

Here is a sampling of what these prophets had to say about or in favour of inclusiveness:

Who sees all beings in his own Self, and his own Self in all beings, loses all fear. (Upanishads, Isa Upanishad)

When one knows God who is hidden in the heart of all things, even as cream is hidden in milk, and in whose glory all things are, he is free from all bondage. (Upanishads, Svetasvatara Upanishad, Part 4)

He who sees the imperishable Supreme Lord residing equally in all perishable living entities, really sees. Seeing Isvara (Lord) equally abiding everywhere, he does not injure the (Greater) Self by the (individual) self, and then attains the Supreme goal. (Gita, 13.27-13.28)

Knowing that the Self exists in all beings, and all beings in the Self, the yogi in union with the Self sees the Self everywhere equally. For him, who sees Me everywhere and everyone, I am not lost; and he is not lost in me. (Gita, 6.29-6.30)

"Then, Kălămas, that noble disciple – devoid of covetnous, devoid of ill will, unconfused, clearly comprehending, ever mindful – dwells pervading one quarter with a mind imbued with loving-kindness, likewise the second quarter, the third, and the fourth. Thus above, below, across, and everywhere, and to all as to himself, he dwells pervading the entire world with a mind imbued with loving-kindness, vast, exalted, measureless, without hostility and without ill will." (Canon, page 90)

And the King shall answer and say unto them, Verily I say unto you, Inasmuch as ye have done it unto one of the least of these my brethren, ye have done it unto me ... Verily I say unto you, Inasmuch as ye did it not to one of the least of these, and ye did it not to me. (Gospels, St. Matthew, Chapter 25, verses 40 and 45)

This is my commandment, That ye love one another, as I have loved you. (Gospels, St. John, Chapter 15, verse 12)

... whoever killed a human being, except as punishment for murder or other villainy in the land, shall be regarded as having killed all mankind; and that whoever saved a human life shall be regarded as having saved all mankind. (Koran, The Table 5, verses 32 and 33)

You people! Have fear of your Lord, who created you from a single soul. From that soul He created its spouse, and through them He bestrewed the earth with countless men and women." (Koran, Women 4, verse 1)

Let him who believes in Allah and the Last Day either speak good or keep silent, and let him who believes in Allah and the Last Day be generous to his neighbour, and let him who believes in Allah and the Last Day be generous to his guest. (Forty Hadith, Hadith 15)

The Master said: "The gentleman, in his attitude toward all under heaven, neither favors anyone nor disfavors anyone. He keeps close to whoever is righteous." (Confucius, 4.10)

He who knows the always-so has room in him for everything; He who has room in him for everything is without prejudice. To be without prejudice is to be kingly; To be kingly is to be of heaven; To be of heaven is to be in Tao. Tao is forever and he that possesses it, Though his body ceases, is not destroyed. (Tao, Chapter 16)

The state of nature has a law of nature to govern it, which obliges every one: and reason, which is that law, teaches all mankind, who will consult it, that being all equal and independent, no one ought to harm another in his life, health, liberty, or possessions: for men being all the workmanship of one omnipotent, and infinitely wise maker

... Every one, as he is bound to preserve himself, and not to quit his station willfully, so by the like reason, when his own preservation comes not in competition, ought he, as much as he can, to preserve the rest of mankind, and may not, unless it be to do justice on another offender, take away, or impair the life, or what tends to the preservation of the life, the liberty, health, limb, or goods of another. (Locke, Two Treatises, Book II, Chapter I)

Everything that destroys social unity is worthless; and all institutions that set man at odds with himself are worthless. (Rousseau, Book IV, Chapter 8)

To promote the little interest of one little order of men in one country, hurts the interest of all other orders of men in that country, and of all men in all other countries. (Rousseau, Book IV, Chapter VII, Part III)

It is not by wearing down into uniformity all that is individual in themselves, but by cultivating it and calling it forth, within the limits imposed by the rights and interests of others, that human beings become a noble and beautiful object of contemplation; and as the works partake the character of those who do them, by the same process human life also becomes rich, diversified, and animating, furnishing more abundant aliment to high thoughts and elevating feelings, and strengthening the tie which binds every individual to the race, by making the race infinitely better worth belonging to. (Mill, Chapter II)

In the place of old bourgeois society, with its classes and class antagonisms, we shall have an association, in which the free development of each is the condition for the free development of all. (Marx & Engels, Manifesto, Chapter 2)

In proportion as the exploitation of one individual by another is put an end to, the exploitation of one nation by another will also be put an end to. In proportion as antagonism between classes within the nation vanishes, the hostility of one nation to another will come to an end. (Marx and Engels, Manifesto, Chapter 2)

Reciprocity: The Sixth Value

The final value for getting along considered in this chapter is reciprocity. Also known as the "Golden Rule", reciprocity is often stated as "do unto others as you would have others do unto you", or sometimes "do *not* do unto others what you do *not* want done unto you."

The idea of reciprocity is also important when considering Rodney King's question. Reciprocity helps reduce conflict by preventing us from demanding privileges for ourselves that we are not willing to accord to others.

Reciprocity enlists the support of others in our beliefs and endeavours, as we promote things that benefit us in a way that benefits everyone.

The absence of reciprocity, on the other hand, can lead to conflict, as our hypocrisy will inevitably attract and justify criticism and more. Hypocrisy leads to disrespect, ridicule and resentment, which lead to anger and violence.

Fortunately reciprocity is largely within our control. We simply need to treat others as we want others to treat us, and accord others the same rights, opportunities and respect that we want for ourselves and our loved ones.

Reciprocity is not without its limitations, however. If I would rather die than eat meat, work on the Sabbath, have an abortion, be homosexual or lose my right to vote, than the doctrine of reciprocity will not prevent me from threatening, abusing, harming or killing those who eat meat, work on the Sabbath, have abortions, are homosexual or want to restrict or take away my right to vote. If I am willing to suffer for my beliefs then reciprocity might give me permission to cause others to suffer for theirs.

Reciprocity by itself, therefore, does not guarantee that we will lead lives free of conflict or suffering.

However, reciprocity combined with tolerance, self-reflection, humility, compassion and inclusiveness, is a different matter. Banded together, this group of values provides a solid base for everyone everywhere to have a chance to lead a life free of conflict, and it will be those who abandon one or more of these values that will stand out as generating the conflict others have to suffer through.

Here are some examples of what some of these prophets said about reciprocity:

By abstaining from the destruction of life, the noble disciple gives to immeasurable beings freedom from fear, hostility, and oppression. By giving to immeasurable beings freedom from fear, hostility, and oppression, he himself will enjoy immeasurable freedom from fear, hostility, and oppression. (Canon, page 173)

The stranger who resides with you shall be to you as one of your citizens; you shall love him as yourself, for you were strangers in the land of Egypt: I the Lord am your God. (Torah, Leviticus, 19.34)

Therefore all things whatsoever ye would that men should do to you, do ye even to them; for this is the law and the prophets. (Gospels, St. Matthew, Chapter 7, verse 12)

And as ye would that me should do to you, do ye also them likewise. (Gospels, St. Luke, Chapter 6, verse 31)

None of you [truly] believes until he wishes for his brother and what he wishes for himself. (Forty Hadith, Hadith 13)

There should be neither harming nor reciprocating harm. (Forty Hadith, Hadith 32)

Zi-gong said: "What I do not wish others to impose on me, I also do not wish to impose on others." (Confucius, 5.12)

'What you do not wish for yourself, do not impose on others.' (Confucius, 12.2)

To understand political power right, and derive it from its original, we must consider, what state all men are naturally in, and that is, a state of perfect freedom to order their actions, and dispose of their possessions and persons, as they think fit, within the bounds of the law of nature ... A state also of equality, wherein all the power and jurisdiction is reciprocal, no one having more than the other; ... (Locke, Book II, Chapter II, section 4)

The sum of all we drive at is that every man may enjoy the rights that are granted to others. (Locke, Letter, page 174)

The citizens all being equal by the social contract, all may prescribe what all must do, instead of nobody having a right to demand that another shall do what he does not do himself. (Rousseau, Social Contract, Book III, Chapter 16)

The only freedom which deserves the name is that of pursuing our own good in our own way, so long as we do not attempt to deprive others of theirs or impede their efforts to obtain it. (Mill, Chapter I)

Common Values for Getting Along

Each of these values by itself can be a powerful tool in avoiding and resolving conflict. The greatest strength of these values, however, is in their synergy. They both empower and temper each other.

Fairly applied they bring balance when the temptation might be to over-balance. They force us to inquire thoughtfully into the causes of conflict until we truly understand them. They require us to reflect upon our own actions and beliefs and consider what is going on inside ourselves as much as what is happening to us.

They provide us with tools by which we can demonstrate a deeper, more equitable and less passionate appreciation of conflict and what can be done to end it. They also provide a basis for challenging and engaging those we are in conflict with.

The values described in this chapter are not surprising or unfamiliar, either alone or in combination.

The insight is the extent to which they are supported across all the prophets considered in this book, from the earliest to the most recent, from East to West, from spiritual to political, and among prophets sometimes perceived as being in conflict with each other.

This insight is of increasing importance as our population soars and strains the planet and we develop and disperse technologies that can easily kill millions as a result of hatred fueled by religious or ideological differences or simple greed, ignorance or negligence.

The common values and collective wisdom identified in this chapter are there to guide those of us who are sincerely trying to find common ground for getting along. They also provide ideological ammunition to use against those who prefer a world of arrogance, hypocrisy or hatred, many of whom have not even read the prophets they rely upon for their worldview or have read them with a selective predisposition.

Surely if we all practiced tolerance, self-reflection, humility, compassion and inclusiveness, did so in a reciprocal fashion, and required our leaders to adhere to these values we would have a world significantly better than the one we have been living in recently, not just for ourselves but for everyone.

Too often we are confronted with rhetoric aimed at our differences.

While differences do exist we also have a great deal in common, as demonstrated by the common values shared by so many of these prophets.

Recognizing and promoting this commonality is an important step in defining global values that we can use to unite rather than divide. Whether this happens or not is up to us, as individuals, families, communities and nations.

5 – Deeds Speak

That actions matter is another theme in the collective teachings of these prophets; that deeds speak louder than words or faith. Again and again the prophets direct us to look at our own behaviour with a critical eye, and to reward or punish others on their behaviour more than their beliefs.

After all, what is most important to us is reflected in our actions, in what we choose to do.

Some behaviour is second nature, we do it without even thinking about it. These actions display our strongest and sometimes most subconscious values. At other times we have to consciously choose between different courses of action. This choice can be difficult when we are torn between two or more important principles.

All of this matters when considering these prophets and what they have to offer in answer to Rodney King's question, as the idea that deeds speak louder than words is one of their most consistent themes. Our actions matter, and matter much more than our words, rhetoric or beliefs, as it is our actions that demonstrate our true values.

Behaviour Matters

No prophet makes the point that deeds speak louder than words, rhetoric, belief or faith more often than the Prophet

Mohammad. It is a theme constantly repeated throughout the Qur'an. Consider this sampling:

Indeed, those that submit to God and do good works shall be recompensed by their Lord: they shall have nothing to fear or regret. (Koran, The Cow, 2:111)

Fear the day you shall all return to God; when every soul shall be paid back for what it did. None shall be wronged. (Koran, The Cow, 2:281)

The day will surely come when each soul shall be confronted with whatever good it did. As for its evil deeds, it will wish they were a long way off. (Koran, The 'Imrams, 3:28)

If you avoid the enormities you are forbidden, We shall pardon your misdeeds and usher you in with all honour ... Men shall be rewarded according to their deeds, and women shall be rewarded according to their deeds. (Koran, Women, 5:30)

Your Lord will surely reward all men according to their deeds. He has knowledge of all their actions. (Koran, Joseph, 11:112)

On that day no soul shall suffer the least injustice. You shall be rewarded according only to your deeds. (Koran, Yā' Sīn, 36:55)

Such is God's promise to His servants who believe and do good works. Say: 'For this I demand of you no recompense. I ask you only to love your kindred. He that does a good deed shall be repaid many times over. God is forgiving and bountiful in His rewards.' (Koran, Counsel, 42:23)

These are rewards for all, according to their deeds, so that He may duly requite them for their works. They shall not be wronged. (Koran, The Sand Dunes, 46:19)

The theme is also continued in The Forty Hadith:

Actions are but by intention and every man shall have but that which he intended (Hadith 1).

O My servants, it is but your deeds that I reckon up for you and then recompense you for, so let him who finds good praise Allah and let him who finds other than that blame no one but himself. (Forty Hadith, Hadith 24)

Whosoever is slowed down by his actions will not be hastened forward by his lineage. (Forty Hadith, Hadith 36)

Mohammad is well supported by most of the other religious prophets in this idea that our actions are what matter most. Here are some examples:

Not every one that saith unto me, Lord, Lord, shall enter into the kingdom of heaven; but he that doeth the will of my Father which is in heaven. (Gospels, St. Matthew, Chapter 7, verse 21)

For what is a man profited, if he shall gain the whole world, and lose his own soul? or what shall a man give in exchange for his soul? For the Son of man shall come in the glory of his Father with his angels; and then he shall reward every man according to his works. (Gospels, St. Matthew, Chapter 16, verses 26-27)

For whosoever shall do the will of God, the same is my brother, and my sister, and my mother. (Gospels, St. Mark, Chapter 3, verse 35).

Not even through deep knowledge can the Atman be reached, unless evil ways are abandoned, and there is rest in the senses, concentration in the mind and peace in one's heart. (Upanishads, Katha Upanishad, Part 2)

According as a man acts and walks in the path of life, so he becomes. He that does good becomes good; he that does evil becomes evil. By pure actions he becomes pure; by evil actions he becomes evil. (Upanishads, The Supreme Teaching, Karma)

The persons, who perform pious and virtuous deeds, and whose sins have come to an end, are free from the delusion of dualities and worship me firmly fixed in their vows. (Gita, 7.28)

"And what, monks, is the Noble Eightfold Path? Right view, right intention, right speech, right action, right livelihood, right effort, right mindfulness, and right concentration." (Canon, page 239)

"Then King Yama says: 'Through negligence, my good man, you have failed to do noble deeds by body, speech, and mind. Well, you will be treated as befits your negligence. That evil action of yours was not done by mother or father, brothers, sisters, friends or companions, nor by relatives, devas, ascetics, or brahmins. But you alone have done that evil deed, and you will have to experience the fruit.'" (Canon, page 29)

" ... it is possible that, by realizing it for himself with direct knowledge, in this very life he will enter upon and dwell in the liberation of mind, liberation by wisdom, that is taintless with the destruction of the taints. Why is that? Because he observes righteous conduct, conduct in accordance with the Dhamma." (Canon, page 161)

"Beings are owners of their actions, heirs of their actions; they originate from their actions, are bound to their actions, have their actions as their refuge. It is action that distinguishes beings as inferior and superior." (Canon, page 166)

It seems that Confucius would also agree. Consider these examples:

When Zi-gong asked about the gentleman, the Master said: "His action goes first; his speech then follows it." (Confucius, 2.13)

The Master said: "The gentleman wishes to be slow in speech but brisk in action." (Confucius, 4.24)

The Master said: "The gentleman deems it shameful if his speech exceeds his action." (Confucius, 14.27)

The Master said: "At first, my attitude toward men was to hear their words and believe in their deeds. Now my attitude toward men is to hear their words and observe their deeds. It was due to Yu that I have changed this." (Confucius, 5.10)

When Zi-zhang asked how to get on in the world, the Master said: "If your speech is wholeheartedly sincere and truthful and your deeds honest and reverent, even in barbarian states, you will get on. If your speech is neither wholeheartedly sincere nor truthful, and your deeds neither honest nor reverent, even in your native place, can you get on?" (Confucius, 15.6)

Even Lao Tzu, who favoured a minimalist approach to action, still left no doubt in how he felt about the relative importance of words and rhetoric:

Those who know do not speak; Those who speak do not know. (Tao, Chapter 56)

True words are not fine-sounding; Fine-sounding words are not true. The good man does not prove by argument; And he who proves by argument is not good. True wisdom is different from much learning; Much learning means little wisdom. (Tao, Chapter 81)

The idea that deeds matter more than words or beliefs is profoundly important in dealing with Rodney King's question of what it takes to get along, especially when combined with the values outlined by the prophets and discussed in previous chapters. The idea applies as much to me as to you, and applies as much to my community as to yours. We should recognize and commend kindred spirits in the actions of others even if they are of different colour, culture, nationality, or political or religious persuasion.

On the other hand, if the actions of others contradict our values or the values they profess, then we must not be fooled by their rhetoric, as we may not have as much in common with them as we think, and the bonds we share might be more illusory than real. Such is the power of actions compared to words.

Finally, in terms of getting along, we must take a look at our own actions, especially as they compare to the values we profess. We must acknowledge and believe that there are things more important than being right, and that one of those things is choosing to do the right thing.

Hypocrisy

To profess values, beliefs or virtues we do not live up to is hypocritical. To demand a standard of others we do not apply to ourselves is hypocritical. As Confucius said, *"hear their words and observe their deeds"* (Confucius, 5.10), in this way we have a chance to recognize hypocrisy in others and in ourselves. Recognizing and dealing with hypocrisy is important in terms of understanding what it takes to get along. Our actions display our true values.

Fine-sounding words and rhetoric can only go so far to darken the spotlight of hypocrisy we often shine upon ourselves.

Hypocrisy ruins our credibility. Hypocrisy erodes the trust others can or should be able place in us. Hypocrisy undermines the persuasive power of the very beliefs we profess. After all, if hypocrites argue for something that they do not live by just how special can that something be?

Challenging hypocrisy is common among the prophets considered in this book, and assailing hypocrisy is a theme that crosses the time, geography and worldviews they represent. Here are some examples:

Those persons, who perform terrible austerities not ordained by the scriptures, given to hypocrisy and ego, impelled by lust, attachment and strength, Mindlessly torturing the multitude of elements in the (physical) body and Me who dwell within the body, know those ignorant ones are of demonic resolve. (Gita, 17.5-17.6)

Judge not, that ye be not judged. For with what judgment ye judge, ye shall be judged; and with what measure ye mete, it shall be measured to you again. Any why beholdest thou the mote that is in thy brother's eye, but considerest not the beam that is in thine own eye? Or how wilt thou say to thy brother, Let me pull out the mote out of thine eye; and, behold, a beam is in thine own eye? Thou hypocrite, first cast out the beam out of thine own eye; and then shalt thou see clearly to cast out the mote out of thy brother's eye. (Gospels, St. Matthew, Chapter 7, verses 1-5)

The hypocrites seek to deceive God, but it is He who deceives them. When they rise to pray, they stand up sluggishly; they pray for the sake of the ostentation and remember God but little, wavering between this and that and belonging neither to these nor those ... The hypocrites shall be cast into the lowest depths of the Fire: there shall be none to help them. (Koran, Women, 4:141 4:146)

... God bears witness that the hypocrites are surely lying. They use their faith as a disguise, and debar others from the path of God. Evil is what they do. They believed and then renounced their faith: their hearts are sealed, so that they are devoid of understanding. When you see them, their good looks please you; and when they speak, you listen to what they say. Yet they are like propped-up beams of timber. Every shout they hear they take to be against them. They are the enemy. Guard yourself against them. God confound them! How perverse they are! [Koran, The Hypocrites, 63:1-63:4)

The Master said: "The reason that the ancients would not rashly utter words is that they deemed it shameful not to live up to them." (Confucius, 4.22)

The Master said: "High-minded yet not straightforward, puerile yet not honest, sincere yet not truthful – I do not understand such people." (Confucius, 8.16)

Whoever will list himself under the banner of Christ, must, in the first place and above all things, make war upon his own lusts and vices. It is in vain for any man to usurp the name of Christ, without holiness of life, purity of manners, benignity and meekness of spirit. (Locke, Letter, page 150)

Now, I appeal to the consciences of those that persecute, torment, destroy, and kill other men upon pretence of religion, whether they do it out of friendship and kindness towards them or no? And I shall then indeed, and not until then, believe they do so, when I shall see those fiery zealots correcting, in the same manner, their friends and familiar acquaintance for the manifest sins they commit against the precepts of the Gospel; when I shall see them persecute with fire and sword the members of their own communion that are tainted with enormous vices and without amendment are in danger of eternal perdition; and when I shall see them thus express their love and desire of the salvation of their souls by the infliction of torments and exercise of all manner of cruelties. For if it be out of principle of charity, as they pretend, and to love men's souls that they deprive them of their estates, maim them with corporal punishments, starve and torment them in noisome prisons, and in the end even take away their lives – I say, if all this be done merely to make men Christians and procure their salvation, why then do they suffer whoredom, fraud, malice, and such-like enormities, which (according to the apostle) manifestly relish of heathenish corruption, to predominate so much and abound amongst their flocks and people? These, and such-like things, are certainly more contrary to the glory of God, to the purity of the Church, and to the salvation of souls, than any conscientious dissent from ecclesiastical decisions, or separation from public worship, whilst accompanied with innocence of life. (Locke, Letter, page 150)

Our merchants and master-manufacturers complain much of the bad effects of high wages in raising the price, and thereby lessening the sale of their goods both at home and abroad. They say nothing concerning the bad effect of high profits. They are silent with regard to the pernicious effects of their own gains. They complain only of those of other people. (Smith, Book I, Chapter IX)

We must never discount the disservice we do to ourselves and the things we hold most dear when our actions do not live up to the very ideals we try to get others to live by.

Leadership

In terms of getting along as communities nothing is more important than ensuring our leaders live up to their rhetoric, not just in promises they make to us but also in how they represent us to others. After all, when they make mistakes, when they fail to deliver, when they bring ridicule, scorn or hostility down on our communities, they are not the only ones who suffer. What they do and what they say on our behalf reflects on all of us.

Our entire country, nation or community can be painted with a brush of frustration or disapproval resulting from the policies or actions of our leaders, affecting us in our daily lives at home or in traveling abroad, if not exposing us to outright danger. And if they are typical of people at the top of most food chains, they may suffer least of all.

It is not unusual for us to discuss a "crisis in leadership" from time to time. It is too bad we rarely discuss a "crisis in followership." In the modern world we are more and more likely to be led by people we choose by ballot or acquiescence. We are more and more likely to get the leadership we deserve.

We must hold those who choose to lead us to a high standard, especially when it comes to actions and hypocrisy. Leaders of all kinds use words to distract us, to cloak themselves in righteousness. However, their actions will display their true values and real integrity. It is through their actions that we must hold them accountable.

Some of the prophets considered in this book were directly concerned with leadership. Others were not concerned with leadership at all. However, here are some of the things these prophets had to say about leaders and leadership:

Whatever a great man does, the other people do. His actions are the only authority, which the whole world follows. (Gita, 3.21)

Heroism, power, determination, resourcefulness, not fleeing from battle, generosity, and leadership are the duty of Kshatriya born of his own nature. (Gita, 18.43)

A wheel-turning monarch, a just and righteous king, who thus provides lawful protection, shelter, and safety for all, is the one who rules by Dhamma only. And that rule cannot be overthrown by any hostile human being. (Canon, page 115)

"'But what, Sire, is the duty of a noble wheel-turning monarch?' – 'It is this, my son: Yourself depending on the Dhamma, honoring it, revering it, cherishing it, doing homage to it, and venerating it, having the Dhamma as your badge and banner, acknowledging the Dhamma as your master, you should establish righteous guard, ward, and protection for your household, your troops, your khattiyas and vassals, for brahmins and householders, town and country folk, ascetics and brahmins, for beasts and birds. Let no crime prevail in your kingdom, and to those who are in need, give wealth. And whatever ascetics and brahmins in your kingdom have renounced the life of sensual infatuation and are devoted to forbearance and gentleness, each one taming himself, each one calming himself, and each one striving for the end of craving, from

time to time approach them and ask: "What, venerable sirs, is wholesome and what is unwholesome, what is blameworthy and what is blameless, what is to be followed and what is not to be followed? What action will in the long run lead to harm and sorrow, and what to welfare and happiness?" Having listened to them, you should avoid what is unwholesome and do what is wholesome. That, my son, is the duty of a noble wheel-turning monarch.' (Canon, page 140)

And whosoever of you will be the chiefest, shall be the servant of all. (Gospels, St. Mark, Chapter 10, verse 44)

For unto whomsoever much is given, of him shall be much required: and to whom men have committed much, of him they will ask more. (Gospels, St. Luke, Chapter 12, verse 48)

Beware of the scribes, which desire to walk in long robes, and love greetings in the markets, and the highest seats in the synagogues, and the chief rooms at feasts: Which devour widows' houses, and for a shew make long prayers; the same shall receive your greater damnation. (Gospels, St. Luke, Chapter 20, verses 46-47)

So after he had washed their feet, and had taken his garments, and was set down again, he said unto them, Know ye what I have done to you? Ye call me Master and Lord: and ye say well, for so I am. If I then, your Lord and Master, have washed your feet; ye also out to wash another's feet. For I have given you an example, that ye should do as I have done to you. (Gospels, St. John, Chapter 13, verses 12-15)

The Master said: "If you govern them with decrees and regulate them with punishments, the people will evade them and will have no sense of shame. If you govern them with virtue and regulate them with rituals, they will have a sense of shame and will flock to you." (Confucius, 2.3)

For a man of humanity is one who, wishing to establish himself, helps others to establish themselves and who, wishing to gain perception, helps others to gain perception. He is able to take himself as an example. This may be called the approach to humanity. (Confucius, 6.30)

Master Zeng said: "Since the sovereign lost the Way, the people have long gone astray. If you get at the truth of a case, have compassion, and do not take delight in it." (Confucius, 19.19)

"Be lenient and you shall win the multitude; be truthful and the people shall trust you; be industrious and you shall score successes; be impartial and the people shall be pleased." (Confucius, 20.1)

The man of highest 'power' does not reveal himself as a possessor of 'power; Therefore he keeps 'power'. The man of inferior 'power' cannot rid it of the appearance of 'power'; Therefore he is in truth without 'power'. (Tao, Chapter 38)

Can you love the people and rule the land, yet remain unknown? Can you in opening and shutting the heavenly gates play always the female part? Can your mind penetrate every corner of the land, but you yourself never interfere? Rear them, feed them, Rear them, but do not lay claim to them. Control them, but never lean upon them; Be chief among them, but do not manage them. This is called the Mysterious Power. (Tao, Chapter 10)

Truly, 'The greatest carver does the least cutting'. (Tao, Chapter 28)

As usurpation is the exercise of power, which another hath right to; so tyranny is the exercise of power beyond right, which no body can have a right to. And this is making use of the power any one has in his hands, not for the good of those who are under it, but for his own private separate advantage. When the governor, however entitled, makes not the law, but his will, the rule; and his commands and actions are not directed to the preservation of the properties of his people, but the satisfaction of his own ambition, revenge, covetnous, or any other irregular passion. (Locke, Two Treatises, Book II, Chapter XVIII)

It is a mistake, to think that this fault is proper only to monarchies; other forms of government are liable to it, as well as that; for wherever the power, that is put in any hands for the government of the people, and the preservation of their properties, is applied to other ends, and made use of to impoverish, harass, or subdue them to the arbitrary and irregular commands of those that have it; there it presently becomes tyranny, whether those that use it are one or many. (Locke, Two Treatises, Book II, Chapter XVIII)

God Almighty grant, I beseech Him, that the gospel of peace may at length be preached, and that civil magistrates, growing more careful to conform their own consciences by human laws, may, like the fathers of their country, direct all counsels and endeavours to promote universally the welfare of all their children, except only as such as are arrogant, ungovernable, and injurious to their brethren; (Locke, Letter, page 175)

To hurt in any degree the interest of any one order of citizens, for no other purpose but to promote that of some other, is evidently contrary that justice and equality of treatment which the sovereign owes to all the different orders of his subjects. (Smith, Wealth, Book II, Chapter VIII)

According to the system of natural liberty, the sovereign has only three duties to attend to; three duties of great importance, indeed, but plain and intelligible to common understandings: first, the duty of protecting the society from violence and invasion of independent societies; secondly, the duty of protecting, as far as possible, every member of the society from the injustice or oppression of every other member of it, or the duty of establishing an exact administration of justice; and thirdly, the duty of erecting and maintaining certain public works and certain public institutions, which it can never be for the interest of any individual, or small number of individuals, to erect and maintain; because the profit could never repay the expence to any individual or small number of individuals, though it may frequently do much more than repay it to a great society. (Smith, Wealth, Book V, Chapter 1, Part III)

In the case of any person whose judgment is really deserving of confidence, how has it become so? Because he has kept his mind open to criticism of his opinions and conduct. Because it has been his practice to listen to all that could be said against him; to profit by as much of it as was just, and to expound to himself, and upon occasion to others, the fallacy of what was fallacious. Because he has felt that the only way in which a human being can make some approach to knowing the whole of a subject is by hearing what can be said about it by persons of a variety of opinion, and studying all modes in which it can be looked at by every character of mind. No wise man ever acquired his wisdom in any mode but this; nor is it in the nature of human intellect to become wise in another manner. (Mill, Chapter II)

To return to Rodney King's question, the issue of leadership must be considered. In terms of getting along, choosing the right leaders to follow, and keeping our leaders on the sort of path charted by these prophets, is something that really matters. To do this, we need to hold them accountable by their actions to their words.

The consequences for not doing so may be felt far more by the people we love than by the leaders who fail us.

Equanimity

Just as important as what we do is the attitude with which do it. Doing the right thing with the wrong spirit can be as damaging to our relationships as if we did not bother to do the right thing to begin with. If doing the right thing is more important than being right, than doing it with the right attitude and spirit is the best statement of all.

As well as the values of tolerance, compassion, non-violence and humility discussed above, some of the prophets considered in this book propose equanimity in doing. The English word for "equanimity" comes from Latin words for "equal" and "mind."

In the context of getting along, equanimity in doing suggests stability, calmness, composure, coolness to the flames of passionate attachment or opinion, reflective of all sides of a question, and to some extent, acceptance of things as they really are. Consider these examples:

Not even through deep knowledge can the Atman be reached, unless evil ways are abandoned, and there is rest in the senses, concentration in the mind, and peace in one's heart. (Upanishads, Katha Upanishad, Part 2)

Having reached that place supreme, the seers find joy in wisdom, their souls have fulfilment, their passions have gone, they have peace. Filled with devotion, they have found the Spirit in all and go into the All. (Upanishads, Muncaka Upanishad, Part 3, Chapter 2)

O Dhananjaya (Arjuna), give up attachment, and remain the same in success and failure. Be steadfast in yoga and do your work. Equanimity (Samatvam) is yoga. (Gita, 2.48)

"Again, a monk dwells pervading one quarter with a mind imbued with compassion ... with a mind imbued with altruistic joy ... with a mind imbued with equanimity, likewise the second, likewise the third, likewise the fourth; so above, below, around, and everywhere, and to all as to himself, he dwells pervading the all-encompassing world with a mind imbued with equanimity, abundant, exalted, immeasurable, without hostility, and without ill will. When the liberation of mind by equanimity is developed in this way, no limiting action remains there, none persists there." (Canon, page 178)

"With the fading away as well of rapture, he dwells equanimous and, mindful and clearly comprehending, he experiences happiness with the body; he enters and dwells in the third jhāna of which the noble ones declare: 'He is equanimous, mindful, and one who dwells happily.' With the abandoning of pleasure and pain, and with the previous passing away of joy and dejection, he enters and dwells in the fourth jhāna, which is neither painful nor pleasant and includes the purification of mindfulness by equanimity. This is called right concentration." (Canon, page 240)

The Master said: "The gentleman, in his attitude toward all under heaven, neither favors anyone nor disfavors anyone. He keeps close to whoever is righteous. (Confucius, 4.10)

As the heavy must be the foundation of the light, So quietness is lord and master of activity. (Tao, Chapter 26)

The blankness of the Unnamed Brings dispassion; To be dispassionate is to be still, And so, of itself, the whole empire will rest. (Tao, Chapter 37)

So he, by his limpid calm, Puts right everything under heaven. (Tao, Chapter 45)

Unlike most other values discussed in this book, equanimity is not widely reflected across the geography or schools of thought of the prophets considered here. It is not easy to find support for "equanimity" in the words of the prophets of modern Western Europe or any of the three Middle Eastern monotheist religions.

In terms of equanimity, the dividing line between East and West is more like the Indus River, with the prophets favouring equanimity lying to the East of the Indus and including the Indian and Chinese philosophers considered here. Perhaps this is one of the differences between East and West that has yet to be widely recognized.

The passions of the Middle East and the West may seem as foreign to those of a Hindu, Buddhist or Chinese tradition as the patience and placidity of the East may seem to those of Western or Monotheist traditions.

However, what matters here is to consider what it takes to get along. In that respect, holding passion in balance must be a good thing. Combined with an emphasis on actions over rhetoric, and a refusal to reward hypocrisy, we have additional insight into what it takes to get along as suggested by many prophets of our combined past.

Positive Commitments for Getting Along: What We Should Do

No single idea presented in the last three chapters will, by itself, ensure that we can get along. However, a powerful system for getting along emerges if we agree with and live by the collective wisdom of these leading prophets.

The strength of this system is not in a single value but in a collection of values whose combined strength is greater than the sum of their individual parts.

This list includes the three sacrifices of freedom, wealth and violence; the six values of tolerance, self-reflection, humility, compassion, inclusiveness and reciprocity; and a commitment to being judged and judging others by actions rather than beliefs, faith or rhetoric.

These are the things we *should* do. These are our positive commitments.

But this is not all the system should include. We also have to consider what we should *not* do. We have to consider our negative commitments.

What these prophets have to say on negative commitments is the subject of the next chapter. In examining them we come at Rodney King's question from a different way. We identify the major vices that keep us from getting along.

Many Prophets, One Wisdom

Chapter 6 - Five Vices

So what holds us back? What keeps us from getting along? Why can't we seem to work things out peacefully?

Based on the teachings already considered we need to live by some key values if we want to get along, including surrender to a higher collective spirit, charity, non-violence, tolerance, self-reflection, humility, compassion, inclusiveness and reciprocity. The absence of these values can create situations of conflict and may help explain why it is difficult for us to get along from time to time.

Admittedly it is difficult to hold to all these values all the time, especially when others around us do not, and especially when we are under attack. But this difficulty is what makes these values important and worthwhile.

That these values are hard to live by in all situations *is* what makes them valuable to begin with.

In terms of more specific guidance on what keeps us from getting along the collective wisdom of these prophets includes five common sources of human strife that I refer to as five vices in this chapter – greed, violence, ignorance, dogmatism and exclusivity.

Greed: The First Vice

The prophets considered in this book advocate a worldview which includes the sacrifice of wealth and an emphasis on charity. It is therefore no surprise that greed is a major factor in their list of sins.

Consider these further examples of what the prophets have to say about greed, a concern that spans time, geography and ideological differences:

The wise who, free from desires, adore the Spirit pass beyond the seed of life in death. A man whose mind wanders among desires, and is longing for objects of desire, goes again to life and death according to his desires. But he who possesses the End of all longing, and whose self has found fulfilment, even in his life desires will fade away. (Upanishads, Munaka Upanishad, Chapter 2)

"I gained this today." "I will fulfill this desire (tomorrow)." "I have this wealth." "Moreover, I am going to gain this later.": This is what they think ... Dependent on their ego, strength, pride, lust, and anger, these envious and indignant people hate Me residing in their own and others' bodies. (Gita, 16.15 and 16.18)

"Kălămas, a person who is greedy, hating, and deluded, overpowered by greed, hatred, and delusion, his thoughts controlled by them, will destroy life, take what is not given, engage in sexual misconduct, and tell lies; he will also prompt others to do likewise. Will that conduce to his harm and suffering for a long time?" – "Yes, venerable sir." (Canon, page 89)

And the cares of this world, and the deceitfulness of riches, and the lusts of other things entering in, choke the word, and it become untruthful. (Gospels, St. Mark, Chapter 4, verse 19)

And he said unto them, Take heed, and beware of covetnous: for a man's life consisteth not in the abundance of the things which he possesseth. (Gospels, St. Luke, Chapter 12, verse 15)

Never let those who hoard the wealth, which God has bestowed on them out of His bounty think it good for them: indeed it is an evil thing for them. The riches they have hoarded shall become their fetters on the Day of

Resurrection. It is God who will inherit the heavens and the earth. God is cognizant of all your actions. (Koran, The 'Imrams, 3.180)

Indeed, the wrongdoers are led unwittingly by their own appetites. And who can guide those whom God has led astray? There shall be none to help them. (Koran, The Greeks, 30:29)

Those that preserve themselves from their own greed shall surely prosper. (Koran, Exile, 59.10)

The Master said: "Acting solely in pursuit of profit will incur much resentment." (Confucius, 4.12)

The Master said: "The gentleman is conversant with righteousness; the small man is conversant with profit." (Confucius, 4.16)

The Master said: "If a man possesses the Duke of Zhou's magnificent talents but is arrogant and stingy, the rest of him is not worth seeing." (Confucius, 8.11)

Those who possess this Tao do not try to fill themselves to the brim, And because they do not try to fill themselves to the brim They are like a garment that endures all wear and need never be renewed. (Tao, Chapter 15)

No lure is greater than to possess what others want, No disaster greater than not to be content with what one has, No presage of evil greater than that men should be wanting to get more. Truly: 'He who has once known the contentment that comes simply through being content, will never again be otherwise than contented'. (Tao, Chapter 46)

The being rightfully possessed of great power and riches, exceedingly beyond the greatest part of the sons of Adam, is so far from being an excuse, much less a reason, for rapine and oppression, which the endamaging another without authority is, that is a great aggravation of it: for the exceeding the bounds of authority is no more a right in a great, than in a petty officer; no more justifiable in a king than a constable; but so much worse in him, in that he has more trust put in him, has already a much greater share than the rest of his brethren, and is supposed, from the advantages of his education, employment, and counselors, to be more knowing in the measures of the right and wrong. (Locke, Book II, Chapter XVIII)

But avarice and ambition in the rich, in the poor the hatred of labour and the love of present ease and enjoyment, are the passions which prompt to invade property, passions much more steady in their operation, and much more universal in their influence. Wherever there is great property, there is great inequality. (Smith, Book V, Chapter I, Part II)

... where wealth is concerned, that no citizen shall be rich enough to buy another and none so poor as to be forced to sell himself; this in turn implies that the more exalted persons need moderation in goods and influence and the humbler persons moderation in avarice and covetousness. (Rousseau, Book II, Chapter II)

At the historical dawn of capitalist production – and every capitalist upstart has personally to go through this historical stage – avarice, and desire to get rich, are the ruling passions. (Marx, Das Kapital, Par VII, Chapter XXIV, Section 4)

Although, therefore, the prodigality of the capitalist never possesses the bonâ-fide character of the open-handed feudal lord's prodigality, but, on the contrary, has always lurking behind it the most sordid avarice and the most anxious calculation, yet his expenditure grows with his accumulation, without the one necessarily restricting the other. (Marx, Das Kapital, Par VII, Chapter XXIV, Section 4)

Based on these selections there appears to be near unanimity among the prophets that greed is a problem, and the sort of problem that can lead to conflict. This thinking leads back to the sacrifice of wealth and the power of humility referred to earlier sections in this book.

Wealth should not be flaunted, wasted or hoarded. Those of us fortunate enough to accumulate some extra wealth must recognize the extent that good fortune and exploitation may have been contributing factors, and take more pride in our ability to quietly and privately give back and share than in our ability to measure our success in currency or what it can buy.

Violence: The Second Vice

In Chapter 3 it was argued that the sacrifice of violence is required in order to get along. That sacrifice may be the single most important element in the foundation of a society.

It follows, therefore, that pursuit of violence is another factor that keeps us from getting along. The inability to create or abide by institutions and doctrines leading to peaceful dispute resolution is an ongoing source of conflict, as one side or another reserves the right and capability to execute violence in pursuit of its goals.

As far as we have come in our humanity, our inability to disarm, at a personal, community or national level, and the need for us to retain weapons of all sorts to preserve our rights of violence from or upon others, is a testament to how far we still have to go.

In addition to the numerous extracts already referred to in Chapter 3 in support of the sacrifice of violence, consider these additional comments from prophets considered in this book:

"Greed, hatred, and delusion of every kind are unwholesome. Whatever action a greedy, hating, and deluded person heaps up – by deeds, words, or thoughts – that too is unwholesome. Whatever suffering such a person, overpowered by greed, hatred, and delusion, his thoughts controlled by them, inflicts under false pretexts upon another – by killing, imprisonment, confiscation of property, false accusations, or expulsion – being prompted in this by the thought, 'I have power and I want power,' all this is unwholesome too." (Canon, page 36)

And Jesus said unto him, Friend, wherefore are thou come? Then came they, and laid hands on Jesus, and took him. And, behold, one of them, which were with Jesus stretched out his hand, and drew his sword, and struck a servant of the high priest's, and smote off his ear. Then Jesus said unto him, Put up again thy sword into his place: for all they that take the sword shall perish with the sword. (Gospels, St. Matthew, Chapter 26, verses 50-52)

When Zi-lu asked about the gentleman, the Master said: "He cultivates himself in reverence." Zi-lu said: "Is that all?" The Master said: "He cultivates in bringing peace to men." Zi-lu said: "Is that all?" The Master said: "He cultivates himself in bringing peace to the hundred family names. To cultivate oneself in bringing peace to the hundred family names – even Yao and Shun found it difficult." (Confucius, 14.42)

Fine weapons are none the less ill-omened things. That is why, among people of good birth, in peace the left-hand side is the place of honour, but in war this is reversed and the right-hand side is the place of honour. The Quietest, even when he conquers, does not regard weapons as lovely things. For to think them lovely means to delight in them, and to delight in them means to delight in the slaughter of men. And he who delights in the slaughter of men will never get what he looks for out of those that dwell under heaven. A host that has slain men is received with grief and mourning; he that has conquered in battle is received with rites of mourning. (Tao, Chapter 31)

He that works through violence may get his way; But only what stays in place Can endure. (Tao, Chapter 33)

The more 'sharp weapons' there are, The more benighted will the whole land grow. (Tao, Chapter 57)

Now 'he who tries to do the master-carpenter's chipping for him is lucky if he does not cut his hand.' (Tao, Chapter 74)

But conquest is as far from setting up any government, as demolishing an house is from building a new one in its place. Indeed, it often makes way for a new frame of commonwealth, by destroying the former; but, without the consent of the people, can never erect a new one. (Locke, Treatises, Book II, Chapter XVI)

That the aggressor, who puts himself into the state of war with another, and unjustly invades another man's right, can, by such an unjust war, never come to have a right over the conquered, will be easily agreed by all men, who will not think, that robbers and pirates have a right of empire over whomsoever they have force enough to master; or that men are bound by promises, which unlawful force extorts from them. (Locke, Treatises, Book II, Chapter XVI)

The injury and the crime is equal, whether committed by the wearer of a crown, or some petty villain. The title of the offender, and the number of the followers, makes no difference to the offence, unless it be to aggravate it. The only difference is, great robbers punish little ones, to keep them in their obedience; but the great ones are rewarded with laurels and triumphs, because they are too big for the weak hands of justice in this world, and have the power in their own possession, which should punish offenders. (Locke, Treatises, Book II, Chapter XVI)

In terms of getting along, violence, the threat of violence, the existence of weapons, and the willingness to threaten to use them, will hold us back.

Furthermore, if we insist on rights of violence we are empowering everyone else, including foe as well as friend, to insist on their own right of violence as well. If we are a perceived as a threat, and even more importantly if it is our goal to be perceived as a threat, how can we object if others respond accordingly? In today's "civilized" world the threat and capability of violence still seem to be necessary evils, especially on an international level. Humanity must address this necessity.

Looking within ourselves through honest self-reflection is a good place to start, whether as individuals, communities or nations. Doing more to support institutions and practices that lead to peaceful resolution of disputes also makes sense. As much as there is evidence all around us that violence is human nature, so too is there a mountain of evidence that much more can be accomplished without violence than with it.

Ignorance: The Third Vice

A third factor that holds us back from getting along is ignorance. However, in ignorance there is hope, for ignorance can be cured. Ignorance is a factor in many of the world's present problems, and more and better education is a ready place to begin solving them. To do that we need to teach people to read and think for themselves.

They must have the tools, training and values to seek out knowledge from a variety of sources. They must have the ability to recognize fallacious reasoning, hypocrisy and sophistry, and consider all sides to a problem. And they must have enough political and moral will and freedom to be able to act upon their conclusions in a peaceful manner.

As well as fear, ignorance is a major weapon in the arsenal of oppression, inequality and exploitation, and nothing threatens an oppressor more than knowledge or education.

The majority of the prophets considered in this book valued knowledge and abhorred ignorance as much as any other quality. Consider these examples:

Abiding in the midst of ignorance, but thinking themselves wise and learned, fools aimlessly go hither and thither, like blind led by the blind. (Upanishads, Mundaka Upanishad, Part 1, Chapter 2)

Desire and hate arise from the dual nature of delusion, O Bharata. (Gita, 7.27)

Even if you are the greatest or worst of sinners of all sinners, you will certainly cross over sins or wickedness by the boat of knowledge or wisdom. (Gita, 4.36)

Greater than the material sacrifice is the sacrifice of knowledge, O Parantapa. All works without exception (kamakhilam) O Partha, attain fulfillment or completion in knowledge or wisdom. (Gita, 4.33)

"There comes a time, monks, when the great ocean dries up and evaporates and no longer exists, but still, I say, there is no making an end of suffering for those beings roaming and wandering on hindered by ignorance and fettered by craving." *(Canon, page 39)*

"And what is ignorance, what is the origin of ignorance, what is the cessation of ignorance, what is the way leading to the cessation of ignorance? Not knowing about suffering, not knowing about the origin of suffering, not knowing about the cessation of suffering, not knowing the way leading to the cessation of suffering – this is called ignorance." *(Canon, page 334)*

"Two things, O monks, partake of true knowledge. What two? Serenity and insight. When serenity is developed, what benefit does one experience? The mind is developed. When the mind is developed, what benefit does one experience? All lust is abandoned. When insight is developed, what benefit does one experience? Wisdom is developed. When wisdom is developed, what benefit does one experience? All ignorance is abandoned." *(Canon, page 267)*

"There are, O monks, these four lights. What four? The light of the moon, the light of the sun, the light of fire, and the light of wisdom. Of these four lights, the light of wisdom is supreme." *(Canon, page 321)*

Many are those that are misled through ignorance by their desires: surely you Lord best knows the transgressors. (Koran, Cattle, 6:119)

Show forgiveness, speak for justice, and avoid the ignorant. If Satan tempts you, seek refuge in God; He hears and knows all. (Koran, The Heights, 7:199)

And while bigotry – the bigotry of ignorance – was holding its sway in the hearts of the unbelievers, God sent down his tranquility on His apostle and on the faithful and made the word of piety binding on them, for they were most worthy and deserving of it. (Koran, Victory, 48:26)

Follow the straight path and do not walk in the footsteps of ignorant men. (Koran, Jonah, 89)

Whoever follows a path to seek knowledge therein, Allah will make easy for him a path to Paradise. (Forty Hadith, Hadith 36)

The Master said: "Do not worry about men not knowing you; rather, worry about incapability and ignorance." (Confucius, 1.16)

Zi-xia said: "To learn extensively and memorize tenaciously; to inquire specifically and think closely – humanity lies therein." (Confucius, 19.6)

Zi-gong asked: "Why was Kong Wen-zi called 'Wen'?" The Master said: "Intelligent and fond of learning, not ashamed to consult his inferiors – that is why he was called 'Wen.'" (Confucius, 5.15)

"To love humanity and not to love learning – the latent defect is foolishness; to love wisdom by not to love learning – the latent defect is unprincipledness; to love truthfulness and not to love learning – the latent defect is harmfulness; to love straightforwardness but not to love learning – the latent defect is impetuosity; to love courage and not to love learning – the latent defect is rebelliousness; to love

staunchness and not to love learning – the latent defect is recklessness." (Confucius, 17.7)

To know when one does not know is best. To think one knows when one does not know is a dire disease. Only he who recognizes this disease is a disease Can cure himself of the disease. The Sage's way of curing disease Also consists in making people recognize their diseases as diseases and thus ceasing to be diseased. (Tao, Chapter 71)

The difference of natural talents in different men is, in reality, much less than we are aware of; and the very different genius which appears to distinguish men of different professions, which grown up to maturity, is not upon many occasions so much the cause as the effect of the division of labour. The difference between the most dissimilar characters, between a philosopher and a common street porter, for example, seems to arise not so much from nature, as from habit, custom, and education. (Smith, Book I, Chapter II)

He who knows only his own side of the case knows little of that. His reasons may be good, and no one may be able to refute them. But if he is equally unable to refute the reasons on the opposite side, it he does not so much as know what they are, he has no ground for preferring either opinion. (Mill, Chapter II)

If ignorance is a source of conflict, pursuit of knowledge should be a path to ending it. Whenever we find ourselves in a conflict situation, whether as individuals, communities or nations, we need to ask ourselves the extent to which our ignorance of others or their ignorance of us is contributing to the conflict, and we must take steps to ensure that a fair exchange of knowledge takes place.

It can never be counter-productive to engage a potential knowledge gap, and to work honestly and earnestly to bridge it. It is said that talk is cheap, which it surely is, especially when the cost of conflict is often measured in human lives and our most fundamental values.

Dogmatism: The Fourth Vice

If knowledge is to be valued and ignorance is to be challenged then dogmatism must be addressed. Nothing impedes our humanity like a closed mind, and there is no greater enemy of knowledge than belief wrapped in arrogance.

Dogmatism is present when we are so entrenched in our own beliefs that we leave absolutely no room for doubt or compromise, or when we are so committed to being right ourselves that everyone else can only be wrong.

Dogmatism is another quality that will hold us back from getting along. If ignorance is a source of conflict, how can we avoid conflict if we take pride in our ignorance and use it as a shield, weapon or badge of honour? The following prophets, while strong in their beliefs, were also secure enough in those beliefs to warn against the dangers of dogmatism:

"Why is it, Master Kaccăn, that ascetics fight with ascetics?" "It is, brahmin, because of the attachment to views, adherence to views, fixation on views, addiction to views, obsession with views, holding firmly to views that ascetics fight with ascetics." (Canon, page 35)

Now something that may be fully accepted out of faith, yet it may be empty, hollow, and false; but something else may not be fully accepted out of faith, yet it may be factual, true, and unmistaken. Again, something may be fully approved of ... well transmitted ... well cogitated ... well pondered, yet it may be empty, hollow, and false; but something else may not be well pondered, yet it may be factual, true, and unmistaken ... it is not proper for a wise man who preserves the truth to come to the definite conclusion: 'Only this is true, anything else is wrong.'" (Canon, page 98)

"Again, a monk is contemptuous and insolent ... adheres to his own views, holds on to them tenaciously, and relinquishes them with difficulty. Such a monk dwells without respect and deference toward the Teacher, the Dhamma, and the Sangha, and he does not fulfill training." (Canon, page 130)

The Master said: "The gentleman is broad-minded, the small man is always narrow-minded." (Confucius, 7.36)

The Master said: "Only the highest of the wise and the lowest of the stupid do not change." (Confucius, 17.2)

... 'the weapon that is too hard will be broken, the tree that has the hardest wood will be cut down.' Truly, the hard and mighty are cast down; the soft and the weak set on high. (Tao, Chapter 76)

If there are any persons who contest a received opinion, or who will do so if law or opinion will let them, let us thank them for it, open our minds to listen to them, and rejoice that there is someone to do for us what we otherwise ought, if we have any regard for either the certainty or the vitality of our convictions, to do with much greater labor for ourselves. (Mill, Book II)

In the case of any person whose judgment is really deserving of confidence, how has it become so? Because he has kept his mind open to criticism of his opinions and conduct. Because it has been his practice to listen to all that could be said against him; to profit by as much of it as was just, and to expound to himself, and upon occasion to others, the fallacy of what was fallacious. Because he has felt that the only way in which a human being can make some approach to knowing the whole of a subject is by hearing what can be said about it by persons of a variety of opinion, and studying all modes in which it can be looked at by every character of mind. No wise man ever acquired his wisdom in any mode but this; nor is it in the nature of human intellect to become wise in another manner. (Mill, Chapter II)

Most of the prophets quoted with respect to dogmatism were also voices in support of equanimity. Their caution against the excess of passionate action is also reflected in their caution against a passionate attachment to our own ideas and beliefs.

As for the rest of the prophets, it is hard to believe that philosophers who collectively advocated values of tolerance, self-reflection and humility, and favoured knowledge over ignorance, would object to a general admonishment against dogmatism and the damage that can be done to human relations by the passionate and obstinate refusal to consider merit in the ideas of others or flaws in our own.

Exclusivity: The Fifth Vice

Exclusivity is the fifth and final consideration in the key impediments to getting along.

We must beware of worldviews that prefer us to others, or open doors for some but not for all. To profess a special insight or privilege and then deny others an opportunity to share that with us is inevitably going to lead to resentment, both from those who want to join us but cannot and from those who do not believe we are that special at all and resent the arrogance of our self-promotion. This is particularly true of religious, spiritual or political beliefs, or economic privileges, built around status, gender, tribe, nationality or race. Surely exclusivity conflicts not only with inclusiveness but also with self-reflection, humility and reciprocity. Here are some further reminders of what these prophets had to say about exclusivity and the inclusive worldview that is their preferred alternative, to add to those set out in Chapter 4:

What is here is also there, and what is there is also here. Who sees the many and not the ONE, wanders from death to death. Even by the mind this truth is to be learned: there are not many but only ONE. Who sees variety and not the unity wanders from death to death. (Upanishads, Katha Upanishad)

Being one with Brahman, the tranquil atma neither laments nor desires, equal to all living beings, he attains Supreme devotion to Me. (Gita, 18.54)

The Supreme Lord resides within the hearts of all living beings, O Arjuna. (Gita, 18.61)

This is my commandment, That ye love one another, as I have loved you. (Gospels, St. John, Chapter 15, verse 12)

The Master said: "The gentleman, in his attitude toward all under heaven, neither favors anyone nor disfavors anyone. He keeps close to whoever is righteous." (Confucius, 4.10)

He who has room in him for everything is without prejudice. To be without prejudice is to be kingly; To be kingly is to be of heaven; To be of heaven is to be in Tao. (Tao, Chapter 16)

But though men, when they enter society, give up the equality, liberty, and executive power they had in the state of nature, into the hands of society, to be so far disposed of by the legislature, as the good of the society shall require; yet it being only with an intention in every one the better to preserve himself, his liberty and property; (for no rational creature can be supposed to change his condition with an intention to be worse) the power of the society, or legislative constituted by them, can never be supposed to extend farther, than the common good; but it is obliged to secure every one's property ... And so whoever has the legislative or supreme power of any commonwealth, is bound to govern be establishing standing laws, promulgated and known to the people, and not be extemporary decrees; by indifferent and upright judges, who are to decide controversies by those laws; and to employ the force of the community at home, only in the execution of such laws, or abroad to prevent or redress foreign injuries, and secure the community from inroads and invasion. And all this to be directed to no other end, but the peace, safety, and public good of the people. (Locke, Two Treatises, Book II, Chapter IX)

To promote the little interest of one little order of men in one country, hurts the interest of all other orders of men in that country, and of all men in all other countries. (Smith, Book IV, Chapter VII, Part III)

In proportion as the exploitation of one individual by another is put an end to, the exploitation of one nation by another will also be put an end to. In proportion as antagonism between classes within the nation vanishes, the hostility of one nation to another will come to an end. (Marx and Engels, Manifesto, Chapter 2)

Negative Commitments for Getting Along: What We Should Not Do

To return to Rodney King's question, greed, violence, ignorance, dogmatism and exclusivity all contribute to the conflicts that prevent us from getting along. There is nothing new in these conclusions or the catalogue of values on which they are based.

What has changed, however, is the world in which we live. Few of us live behind natural or unnatural barriers we can defend from all comers. Airplanes, helicopters, telephones, cell phones, televisions, radio signals, satellites, viruses, bacteria, missiles, nuclear radiation, population pressure, pollution, global warming and the Internet, among others, conspire to ensure that there are no more islands in the literal or figurative sense.

To create a world in which we hold all the power and receive all the benefits to the exclusion of the rest of humanity within or without our own nation is just not realistic in the modern world. Sooner or later others will want in, or those within will want out, and often for good reason. Sooner or later the riches or privilege we enjoy off the backs of the less fortunate will lead to our downfall.

Sooner or later someone stronger will come along, or a natural catastrophe will require us to seek help from others. Sooner or later we will want to share in a commodity produced somewhere else, or a technology developed elsewhere, that we cannot afford to be without. Surely the values suggested by these prophets are the better approach, not just in their ancient and historical world but even more so in the modern, inter-connected world of the 21st century.

7 – The Prophets on Enemies

There has rarely been a good time in human history to be classified as anyone's "enemy." This is particularly true as we move deeper into the 21st century. The technology of war has never been more effective, available and one-sided.

Many of the military, political, and moral battles of the past few hundred years, including the horrific cataclysm of World War II, were fought to create safe havens, either in physical place or international convention.

Since 9/11, however, many of those save havens have been attacked or eroded, and the countries doing the attacking include countries that hold themselves out as bastions of democracy and tolerance.

Citizens of Western liberal democracies cannot even consider their own countries safe havens anymore as panicked governments have trampled human rights and civil liberties in their stampede for political righteousness and national security.

If power corrupts than nothing seems to corrupt commonsense, humanity and compassion more than power over ones "enemies," whether on the streets of Rwanda or the killing fields of Cambodia; from the air against numerous World War II cities including Warsaw, London, St. Petersburg, Berlin, Munich, Dresden, Tokyo, Hiroshima or Nagasaki; or in countless places around the world in the past century.

If there are key values that really matter in terms of getting along, and if hypocrisy is a clear example of inconsistency leading to conflict, how we perceive and deal with our enemies must be important when attempting to answer Rodney King's question.

Some of the prophets considered in this book have given thought and guidance on how to treat enemies. The monotheist prophets, in particular, have had a lot to say on how to treat enemies.

Consider these examples from the books of Deuteronomy and Numbers in the Torah, which are also two of the first books in the Christian Old Testament:

When you approach a town to attack it, you shall offer it terms of peace. If it responds peaceably and lets you in, all the people present there shall serve you at forced labor. If it does not surrender to you, but would join battle with you, you shall lay siege to it; and when the Lord God delivers it unto your hand, you shall put all its males to the sword. You may, however, take as your booty the women, the children, the livestock, and everything in the town – all its spoil – and enjoy the use of the spoil of your enemy, which the Lord God gives to you. (Torah, Deuteronomy, Chapter 20, verses 20.10-20.14)

When the Lord your God brings you to the land that you are about to enter and possess, and He dislodges many nations before you – the Hittites, Girgashites, Amorities, Canaanites, Perizzites, Hivites, and Jebusites, seven nations much larger than you – and the Lord God delivers them to you and you defeat them, you must doom them to destruction: grant no terms and give them no quarter. (Torah, Deuteronomy, Chapter 7, verses 7.1-7.2)

And the Lord said to me: See, I begin by placing Sihon and his land at your disposal. Begin the occupation; take possession of his land. Sihon with all his men took the field against us at Jahaz, and the Lord God delivered him to us and we defeated him and his sons and all his men. At that time we captured all his towns, and we doomed every town – men, women and children – leaving no survivor. (Torah, Deuteronomy, Chapter 2, verses 2.31-2.34)

So the Lord God also delivered into our power King Og of Bashan, with all his men, and we dealt them such a blow that no survivor was left. At that time we captured all his towns; there was not a town that we did not take from them: sixty towns, the whole district of Argob, the kingdom of Og in Bashan – all those towns fortified with high walls, gates, and bars – apart from a great number of unwalled towns. We doomed them as we had done in the case of the King of Sihon of Hesbon: we doomed every town – men, women and children – and retained as booty all the cattle and the spoil of the towns. (Torah, Deuteronomy, Chapter 3, verses 3.3-3.7)

They took the field against the Midian, as the Lord had commanded Moses, and slew every male ... The Israelites took the women and children of the Midianites captive, and seized as booty all their beasts, all their herds, and all their wealth. And they destroyed by fire all the towns in which they were settled, and their encampments ... Moses, Eleazar the priest, and all the chieftains of the community came out to meet them outside the camp. Moses became angry with the commanders of the army, the officers of thousands and the officers of hundreds, who had come back from the military campaign. Moses said to them, "You have spared every female!, Yet they are the very ones who, at the bidding of Balaam, induced the Israelites to trespass against the Lord in the matter of Peor, so that the Lord's community was struck by plague. Now, therefore, slay every woman who has known a man carnally; but spare every young woman who has not had carnal relations with a man ... The amount of booty, other than the spoil that the troops had plundered, came to 675,000 sheep, 72,000 head of cattle, 61,000 asses, and a total of 32,000 human beings, namely, the women who had not had carnal relations. (from Numbers 31, verses 1 to 35)

The Gospels, which are the first four books of the Christian New Testament, take a very different approach to treatment of enemies. Consider these examples:

Ye have heard it hath been said, An eye for an eye, and a tooth for a tooth; But I say unto you, That ye resist not evil: but whosoever shall smite thee on thy right cheek, turn to him the other also. (Gospels, St. Matthew, Chapter 5, verses 38-39)

Ye have heard that it hath been said, Thou shalt love thy neighbour, and hate thine enemy. But I say unto you, Love your enemies, bless them that curse you, do good to them that hate you, and pray for them which despitefully use you, and persecute you; That ye may be the children of your Father which is in heaven: for he maketh his sun rise on the evil and on the good, and sendeth rain on the just and the unjust. For if ye love them which love you, what reward have ye? do not even the publicans the same? And if ye salute your brethren only, what do ye more than others? do not even publicans do so? Be ye therefore perfect, even as your Father which is in heaven is perfect. (Gospels, St. Matthew, Chapter 5, verses 43-48)

But I say unto you which hear, Love your enemies, do good to them which hate you, Bless them that curse you, and pray for them which despitefully use you. (Gospels, St. Luke, Chapter 6, verses 27-28)

But love ye enemies, and do good, and lend, hoping for nothing again; and your reward shall be great, and ye shall be the children of the Highest; for He is kind unto the unthankful and to the evil. Be ye therefore merciful, as your Father also is merciful. Judge not, and ye shall not be judged; condemn not, and ye shall not be condemned: forgive, and ye shall be forgiven; (Gospels, St. Luke, Chapter 6, verses 35-37)

The Qur'an contains a combination of both the Torah and Gospel approaches, with its disapproval of initial aggression, exhortation to total war when the enemy is engaged, but openness to peaceful settlement at any time if the opportunity arises to end hostilities in a way which preserves the supremacy Islam for its followers. Consider these examples:

Fight for the sake of God those that fight against you, but do not attack them first. God does not love aggressors. (Koran, The Cow, 2:190)

Permission to take up arms is hereby given to those who are attacked, because they have been wronged. God has power to grant them victory: those who have been unjustly driven from their homes, only because they said: 'Our Lord is God.' (Koran, Pilgrimage, 22:38)

Fight against such of those to whom the Scriptures were given as believe in neither God nor the Last Day, who not forbid what God and His apostle have forbidden, and do not embrace the true Faith, until they pay tribute out of and are utterly subdued. (Koran, Repentance, 9:29)

If you do not go to war, He will punish you sternly, and will replace you by other men. (Koran, Repentance, 9:39)

Believers, make war on the infidels who dwell around you. Deal firmly with them. Know that God is with the righteous. (Koran, Repentance, 9:123)

When you meet the unbelievers in the battlefield strike off their heads and, when you have laid them low, bind your captives firmly. Then grant them freedom or take a ransom from them, until War shall lay down her burdens. (Koran, Muhammad, 47:4)

Tell the unbelievers that if they mend their ways their past shall be forgiven; but if they persist in sin, let them reflect upon the fate of bygone nations. Make war on them until idolatry shall cease and God's religion shall reign supreme. If they desist, God is cognizant of all their actions; but if they pay no heed, know then that God will protect you. (Koran, The Spoils, 8:39-8:40)

Let not the unbelievers think they will ever get away. They have not the power to do so. Muster against them all the men and cavalry at your command, so that you may strike terror into the enemy of God and your enemy, and others besides them who are unknown to you but known to God. All that you give in the cause of God shall be repaid to you. You shall not be wronged. (Koran, The Spoils, 8:59-8:60)

If they incline to peace, make peace with them, and put your trust in God. It is surely He who hears all and knows all. (Koran, The Spoils, 8:61)

Do not make God, when you swear by Him, a means to prevent you from dealing justly, from guarding yourselves against evil, and from making peace among men. (Koran, The Cow, 2:224)

Some of the non-monotheist prophets also had something to say on enemies and treatment of enemies, over and above what they might have said about non-violence, tolerance, compassion and inclusiveness. Consider these examples:

I am the same in all living beings. No one is despicable or dear to me. Those persons who worship Me with devotion are in Me, and I am certainly in them. Even the one, who commits the most sinful acts, is engaged in worship with exclusive devotion to Me, must be thought of as a sadhu, because he is rightly resolved. (Gita, 9.29-9.30)

He who is equable (alike) to a foe and a friend, also to honor and dishonor, in cold and heat, in pleasure and pain, who is free from attachment, equal in defamation and praise, silent, content with anything, having no home, with firm mind, that man is a devotee and dear to Me. (Gita, 12.18-12.19)

Monks, even if bandits were to sever you savagely limb by limb with a two-handled saw, he who gave rise to a mind of hate toward them would not be carrying out my teaching. Herein, monks, you should train thus: 'Our minds will remain unaffected, and we shall utter no bitter words; we shall abide compassionate for their welfare, and a mind of loving-kindness, never in a mood of hate. We shall abide pervading them with a mind imbued with loving-kindness; and starting with them, we shall abide pervading the all-encompassing with a mind of imbued loving-kindness, abundant, exalted, immeasurable, without hostility, and without ill will.' That is how you should train, monks. (Canon, page 279)

Some said: "'Requite enmity [hostility] with favor.' What do you think of that?" The Master said: "Then, how do you requite favor? Requite enmity [hostility] with impartiality; requite favor with favor." (Confucius, 14.34) [Definition added]

Therefore a good general effects his purpose and then stops; he does not take further advantage of his victory. Fulfils his purpose and does not glory in what he had done; Fulfils his purpose and does not boast of what he has done; Fulfils his purpose, but takes no pride in what he has done; Fulfils his purpose, but only as a step that could not be avoided. Fulfils his purpose, but without violence; For what has a time of vigour also has a time of decay. This is against Tao. And what is against Tao will soon perish. (Tao, Chapter 30)

Even in the midst of war, a just prince, seizing what he can of the public property in the enemy's territory, nevertheless respects the persons and possessions of private individuals; he respects the principles on which his own rights are based. Since the aim of war is to subdue a hostile state, a combatant has the right to kill the defenders of that state while they are armed; but as soon as they lay down their arms and surrender, they cease to be enemies or instruments of the enemy; they simply become men once more, and no one has any longer the right to take their lives. It is sometimes possible to destroy a state without killing a single one of its members, and war gives no right to inflict any more destruction than is necessary for victory. These principles ... are derived from the nature of things; they are based on reason. (Rousseau, Book I, Chapter 4)

In conclusion, however, it cannot be said that these prophets have a collective, common wisdom on war and the treatment of enemies. They all wrote at a time when war was considered an inevitable part of the human condition and the end of war was inconceivable.

They also lived before the technology of war had developed to the point of extreme if not total one-sided destruction, and before the technology of communication allowed everyone to see what war was really doing to ordinary people in real time.

However, the values for getting along promoted by these prophets have an important role in dealing with these questions, both in determining who our enemies are and in framing our response to them.

They teach us to be mindful of the sacrifices we need to make in order to get along in a peaceful world – freedom, wealth and violence. They teach us six universal values for getting along – tolerance, self-reflection, humility, compassion, inclusiveness and reciprocity. They remind us that our deeds speak louder than our words, that hypocrisy matters, and that we have to avoid the five universal vices – greed, violence, ignorance, dogmatism and exclusivity.

The difficulty we have holding to such values when faced with true enemies is in itself a testament to their importance. Abandoning these values when we need them the most can undo centuries of human development and return us to the natural order of things where fear and force rule the world.

In terms of war and enemies, we also need to ask ourselves: "Why do we have enemies at all?" and "How can we avoid making enemies to begin with?" The values proposed by these prophets can be profound in helping to answer these questions. They suggest we might not have enemies, or at least would have a lot more friends than enemies, if we simply lived the ideas of non-violence, compassion, open-mindedness and inclusiveness before any conflict arose.

If we were less dogmatic, less exclusive, more accepting, more aware, more inquiring and less judgmental; if we were more tolerant and accepting of diversity. If we were as conscious of the negative effect we have and others as we are of the negative effect others have on us. If we were as convinced of our own fallibility and the fallibility of our prophets as were convinced in the fallibility of others.

Confucius put it this way:

If a gentleman conducts himself with reverence and does nothing amiss, if he treats others with respect and courtesy, all men within the four seas are his brothers. Why should the gentleman worry about having no brothers? (Confucius, 12.5)

Most of us may think that we already live this way, that there is nothing wrong with us and everything wrong with someone else. We have to ask ourselves if this is a fair and realistic worldview, especially if we are repeatedly or continuously in conflict with those around us.

Repeated or continuous conflict might mean we are the only good guy on the street standing between the bad buys and anarchy, or it might mean we do not live the principles we espouse as much as we think we do. It surely cannot hurt to take a hard look at this latter possibility before becoming too convinced of the former.

If civilization as an idea means anything it must mean a state of human affairs where might is no longer right. Perhaps one great contribution to human thought in the past century has been the expanding belief that the end of war is an achievable goal.

Clearly much more work needs to be done. Defining, institutionalizing and living by the common values of peace contained in the collective works of our common prophets can be a good place to start.

8 - What Really Matters

So what can we learn from all this? What can be taken away after spending so much time with these special and influential thinkers? What is it that really matters when it comes to getting along?

Here are some of my thoughts and conclusions, although my hope is you will have new ideas of your own by this stage in the book and will already be seeking out the words of the prophets to read for yourself.

Opportunity to live our lives the way we want

The first thing that really matters is that we all have an opportunity to live our lives the way we want to live them, free of conflict. This must be subject to reasonable limits, including limitations around our mental and physical abilities; the accidents of genetics, disease, illness and inheritance; the geography, climate, and social, economic and political condition of the nation in which we are born or live; and the limitations other nations may impose on our ability to live wherever we want.

We must also be prepared and permitted to work for change in our lives and in our communities within the laws of that community and with respect for the wishes of the majority, as long as those laws do not prevent us from trying to strike out to a place more to our liking if the opportunity arises; apply equally to everyone; impose the fewest restrictions necessary to promote and maintain the core values we all must have if we are going to get along, including non-violence, tolerance, reciprocity, compassion, knowledge and accountability for actions; and provide reasonable protection against the vices that are most likely to lead to conflict, including hypocrisy, greed, violence, ignorance, dogmatism and exclusivity.

If there is any purpose to getting along it must be to free us from conflict and the fear of conflict so that we can pursue things that really matter to us, things more productive and fulfilling, not just for ourselves but for our families and communities.

Offer the same opportunity to everyone

The second thing that really matters is that we provide the same opportunity to others to live their lives they way they want, also free of conflict. This represents the best chance we all have to live our lives the way we want. It is not only the collective wisdom of the prophets we hold most dear, it is a logical extension of self-interest and common sense.

The time will come when we or our loved ones or our nations will be threatened by things we cannot handle on our own. The threat may be natural or human. It may be something unique to our part of the world, spreading from somewhere else, or a challenge to the whole planet.

Or, the time may come when something developed by someone far away is of vital interest to us or our families or our communities, such as a method, technology or cure which can alleviate suffering. Whatever it is, a threat or an opportunity, it is inevitable. Our chances of dealing with it or sharing in it are directly proportional to the number of other people who step up and support us, and that in turn may be directly related to the number or other people we have supported in the past.

If we want to carve out a place where we can live our lives the way we want without conflict and with only reasonable limitation, then we have a much better chance of succeeding if we do that with the support of billions of other people.

However, not all those people are going to want to live exactly the way we want to, and not all those people are going to believe everything we believe, no matter how much we may want them to. Their reason to help us will have to be built on something we all can support. The prophets considered in this book have helped show us what that platform could look like. It is based on the values set out in previous chapters. It should not matter where anyone's belief in those values comes from, whether based on divinity, nature, reason, law, humanity or common sense, as long as the values are shared and work for all, not just for some. History proves those who take by force today are themselves taken by force tomorrow. That too is inevitable.

If we really care to live our life the way we want without conflict, and if you really care that our children and grandchildren have that opportunity as well, then working to provide the same opportunity to other people in other places is what really matters.

If we really care about our suffering and the suffering within our community, then we better really care about the suffering of others and the suffering in their communities. In all these cases it is not doctrine that must carry the day, but significant common values that apply to all and work for all. The modern world leaves us no real alternative.

Another thing that really matters is that we pool our collective wisdom to determine the best way of providing everyone with the same opportunity to live their lives the way they want. We need to stop listening to only the loudest voice in our part of the world, and must start listening to the voices others are listening to as well.

Consider the wisdom of all the world's prophets, and find a common wisdom for all humanity

We must recognize that none of us has all the answers for all the questions for all time, but that by pooling our collective wisdom we can collate the learning of thousands of years and billions of people.

In doing so we should find that we have far more in common than we had ever thought. It is this common ground that creates the building site for a peaceful, threat-free, healthy and prosperous opportunity for each of us and those we love the most. It is not by shutting out or shouting down that this opportunity is created. It comes from finding the best in what we each have to offer. It comes from fairly and honestly reflecting on whether everything we believe, say or do is truly the best idea for everyone, everywhere, all the time.

In this respect our most influential prophets represent a base upon which common ground can be found. Collectively they support common values that are the basis for getting along. We should hold ourselves to these values as vigorously as we insist that others should be held to them as well.

Attack ignorance and dogmatism

Ignorance is a common root to most of the world's evils. We must be even more committed to ending ignorance than we are to ending poverty, hunger, disease, environmental destruction, war, violence, discrimination and other evils. After all, how can we expect to make any serious and lasting headway on such problems if we do not attack ignorance with even greater vigour? Ending ignorance really matters, in us and in others. In attacking ignorance we must not allow ideology to get in the way. We must recognize that ideological ignorance is as great a threat as any ideology. History is littered with ideologues who twisted wisdom to support an agenda for which it was never intended.

We need to challenge those who profess an ideology to prove they truly understand what their own prophets have said. We must challenge those who profess an ideology to allow others to learn and understand it. We must challenge those of us who are so committed to our own beliefs that we fail to learn about or recognize the good in other ideologies or the potential harm in our own. We must also challenge our own ignorance.

Continue to consider what it takes to get along

Another thing that really matters is that we continue to think and talk about what it takes to get along. The world and our understanding of it are constantly changing. We cannot allow our worldviews to become frozen in time. We cannot count on prophets from an age when the planet was dark and empty to have the final word on issues such as reproductive sciences, space exploration, nuclear weapons, biological weapons, natural resource conservation, global warming or any of a multitude of issues they might not have been able to imagine. They may have something to say of relevance, but they may also have nothing helpful to say at all.

We must not end the collective dialogue about what really matters. If we do, we risk creating or maintaining unnecessary suffering for billions, and not just for our fellow human beings but for all the living things on the planet. Answers change as questions change, and the questions have changed dramatically with population growth, climate change, and greater technological capability and scientific understanding.

If we are going to properly frame the questions so we can get answers that are right for our time then we must collate those common values that have passed the test of time. We must identify the values we need to carry forward. We must pull values from the past that are right for the age in which we live today and will endure for some time to come. We must be willing to discard or soften values which are outdated or no longer work. We need to be responsible for our values. We have the power to choose them. We need to choose them wisely.

Do not allow the few to define the many

Another thing that really matters is that we not allow the few to define the many, not only the agenda the many pursues but also what the many believe and how they behave. The prophets considered in this book advocated an inclusive and all encompassing worldview. This inevitably leads to consideration of and respect for the needs and concerns of the greatest majority. In order to do that it is the needs and concerns of ordinary people that matters most.

Too often history is seen through the eyes of the few. The lives of the majority are simply backdrops to a play in which the few are the principal players. It is the stories of the few that are recorded for posterity or dominate contemporary media. The great events of history are often nothing more than suffering and hardship inflicted on the many in conflicts between or caused by the few. This becomes less and less acceptable and more and more extreme as the planet fills with people. Our jostling more easily ripples around the globe. With technology, the ripples move faster, happen more often, and have deadlier potential for the many.

It was nineteen men who hijacked and crashed those planes on September 11th, 2001. Despite the largest manhunt in world history only a handful of others have been implicated in the attack. Yet millions more than originally perished in that despicable attack have borne some of the consequences. The majority have allowed the few, including the 9/11 attackers and those who inspired and funded them and the leaders of Western countries who responded most stridently to their actions, to destabilize and politicize an entire planet. Less than a few dozen people have been the main players in a story that has affected hundreds of millions and killed, maimed, terrorized, imprisoned, displaced or traumatized uncounted thousands.

History is full of such stories. What most often is untold are the countless interactions between billions of people who find a way to live with and support each other on a daily basis with tolerance and compassion and without greed or violence. They may not always like or respect each other, but they manage to work things out anyway. We need institutions, attitudes and values that reflect and protect our collective needs and which do not permit the few to inflict suffering on the many, nor cause the many to abandon the values which make their daily living possible, values like those advocated by the prophets considered in this book.

Above all this, however, we each need to commit to being members of the many and not the few. We each need to commit to applying those values that benefit the many every day of our lives, for our families, our communities, our nations and ourselves. We each need to demand that our leaders do the same.

Demand more of our leaders – and ourselves

A final thing that really matters is that we demand more of our leaders, including those we elect and those who self-elect. We must not permit them to hijack our values and beliefs and use them for a purpose for which they were never intended. We must not permit them to be selective about which of our most important values and beliefs they will live by. We must not permit them to act in sinister and malevolent ways while hiding behind a mask of righteousness. We must not permit them to pull the rug out from under our most important values in the name of protecting those values from attack.

The legacy of our combined prophets is that values, beliefs and behaviours all matter. Their consistent and fair application should be something that really matters.

Let us be unanimous in our determination to end suffering for all without causing suffering to any, and require our leaders to do the same.

Let us remind our leaders that the only ideologies that really matter are those that give us a chance to live our lives as we wish in prosperity and free of conflict without causing suffering to others. After all, if our leaders cannot set the highest possible standard for us all to follow, why do they deserve to be our leaders at all?

9 - The Common Works of Humankind

This book began with a quotation from a speech by Senator Robert F. Kennedy included in the following:

Everywhere new technology and communications brings men and nations closer together, the concerns of one inevitably become the concerns of all. And our new closeness is stripping away the false masks, the illusion of differences which is at the root of injustice and hate and war. Only earthbound man still clings to the dark and poisoning superstition that his world is bounded by the nearest hill, his universe ends at river's shore, his common humanity is enclosed in the tight circle of those who share his town or his views and the color of his skin.

The speech was given in June, 1966, more than forty years before I began the exploration that is ending with these pages. He delivered this speech at the University of Cape Town at a time when apartheid was still in place in South Africa. European colonization had just been abandoned in Africa and Asia. The Cold War was raging. Civil liberties were still awakening in America and the rest of the Western world. It was a Day of Affirmation at the University of Cape Town.

His speech contained an eloquent plea for personal courage and responsibility during a time of great turbulence:

It is from numberless diverse acts of courage such as these that the belief that human history is thus shaped. Each time a man stands up for an ideal, or acts to improve the lot of others, or strikes out against injustice, he sends forth a tiny ripple of hope, and crossing each other from a million different centers of energy and daring those ripples build a current which can sweep down the mightiest walls of oppression and resistance.

It also contained a passage eerily prescient, considering the world events since September 11th, 2001 that inspired me to commence the study that is now this book:

Nations, like men, often march to the beat of different drummers, and the precise solutions of the United States can neither be dictated nor transplanted to others, and that is not our intention. What is important however is that all nations must march toward increasing freedom; toward justice for all; toward a society strong and flexible enough to meet the demands of all of its people, whatever their race, and the demands of a world of immense and dizzying change that face us all.

The journey I took in researching and writing this book owes as much to this speech as it does to the question posed by Rodney King.

In re-reading Senator Kennedy's speech today, of which only a few paragraphs have been extracted here, it is poignant to note that his remarks are as relevant, truthful and insightful today as they were forty years ago. This is sad, in a way, as it means the world has not progressed too far in two generations. However it is also appropriate when considering a lineage of prophets going back thousands of years whose own words are also as relevant today as when they were first spoken. Perhaps Senator Kennedy would refer me to the following passage in his speech, as an answer to that reflection:

Each nation has different obstacles and different goals, shaped by the vagaries of history and of experience. Yet as I talk to young people around the world I am impressed not by the diversity but by the closeness of their goals, their desires, and their concerns and their hope for the future. There is discrimination in New York, the racial inequality of apartheid in South Africa, and serfdom in the mountains of Peru. People starve to death in the streets of India; a former Prime Minister is summarily executed in the Congo; intellectuals go to jail in Russia; and thousands are slaughtered in Indonesia; wealth is lavished on armaments everywhere in the world. These are different evils; but they are the common works of man. They reflect the imperfections of human justice, the inadequacy of human compassion, the defectiveness of our sensibility toward the sufferings of our fellows; they mark the limit of our ability to use knowledge for the well-being of our fellow human beings throughout the world. And therefore they call upon common qualities of conscience and indignation, a shared determination to wipe away the unnecessary sufferings of our fellow human beings at home and around the world.

While there are a variety of different evils at work in our world today, some of which have been around for millennia, the truth and reality is they are all common works of humankind. Every nation has its times of violence, repression, inhumanity and dogmatism to reflect upon, both within its community and inflicted on others around it. For some nations these ill times are more current than others, but all are well documented if anyone cares to look.

Fortunately there are common responses to these evil works as well, based on wisdom, sacrifice, compassion, charity, tolerance and open-mindedness. No-one has cornered the market on goodness or evil, and no-one is likely to do so in the foreseeable future. This is one thing we all share.

We must also resist the temptation to fight evil with evil. What we categorize as evil when enflamed with passion and rhetoric may not be so evil when considered in the calm light of compassion and humility, or when looking honestly into our own history.

When we give ourselves permission to do evil to others we do evil to the very principles we think the world should live by. We suggest to the world that our goodness is a mere veneer. We cause people to question our integrity and leadership, and leave them hoping and searching for a better way. We give them permission to reject the leadership we offer and encourage them to try following a different way.

We must also remember that there are positive and hopeful works which are also the common works of humankind. These include ten thousand years of compassionate observing, learning, thinking and teaching about what really matters and what it takes to get along, some of which has been reflected in the words of the prophets considered in this book. This body of thinking is also our common work. It is not and never will be complete. None of these prophets should be considered the complete or the last word either individually or collectively.

Things can and do change for the better. Ordinary people holding true to values that resonate with everyone can make a difference. Slavery was an accepted institution everywhere for as long as humankind could remember. It became a powerful and important industry. It was eradicated in less than a century through the work of ordinary people who recognized the hypocrisy of slavery when compared to modern values and who recognized the common humanity in all of us. There is no reason why we cannot do the same with war, terrorism and the use or threat of violence to resolve conflict. There is no reason why nuclear, biological and chemical weapons cannot be as discarded as the chains, shackles and whips of the slave trade.

When I began my research I hoped to discover universality among our prophets, total agreement on key levers for breaking barriers and building bridges. I cannot say I found unanimity. But I did find a pool of collective wisdom. A common direction in what we have to do in order to get along. While not all the prophets said all the things necessary to support each and every value their collective wisdom still adds up to a powerful and inspiring message that can unite far more than it divides if we simply choose to see it and use it that way.

Perhaps it is not the answer to Rodney King's question that matters anyway, but the question itself. That we collectively recognize not even the wisest among us has a single answer that will apply to everyone, everywhere, all the time and for all time. Perhaps we need to realize that everyone has a piece of the answer but no-one has the whole answer, and it is only by listening honestly and fairly to ourselves and engaging others with compassion and humility that we can stitch together what is needed for our time and place.

Perhaps one thing that really matters is that we each take responsibility for asking the question of ourselves, our neighbours and our leaders, and keep the question in the forefront of our daily living. How we each choose to answer this question says more about us than anything else, and makes a difference every day both for ourselves and others in the present and also for others and ourselves in the future.

There is something going on in our time we have called globalization. What began as a term applying to international commerce and world trade has changed. Globalization is now a social and political force. A common human experience and common way of life is developing. This process is accelerating with our growth in population and changes in technology.

A consideration of 21st century globalization results in two inevitable conclusions – we all have more in common and we are all more connected than we had ever before imagined. We can see, often in real time, that what I do here affects you over there and what you do over there affects me over here.

These developments require us to discuss and define common, global values to guide and support our increasing interconnectivity and increasingly common experience. There is no better place to begin that process than with the wisdom of past prophets still highly influential in today's world; and for those genuinely interested there is no better way to commence an individual inquiry into their thinking and ideas than to read the teachings of these prophets for themselves.

As a final thought from this inquirer - perhaps the greatest opportunity represented by globalization is the opportunity to entrench on a worldwide basis our collective commitment to a belief eloquently expressed in the English language almost four hundred years ago and supported by so many of our most important prophets:

No man is an Iland, intire of it selfe; every man is a peece of the Continent, a part of the maine; if a Clod bee washed away by the Sea, Europe is the lesse, as well as if a Promontorie were, as well as if a Mannor of thy friends or of thine owne were; any mans death diminishes me, because I am involved in Mankinde; And therefore never send to know for whom the bell tolls; It tolls for thee.

John Donne, England, 1623

Where is the threat in such a sentiment?

What harm is caused by such a belief?

What harm do we do to ourselves and others if we deny it?

1992 Revisited

We've got to get quit, we've got to quit ... it's just not right ... Please, we can get along here, we can all get along here. We're stuck here for while. Let's try and work it out. Let's try and work it out.

Rodney King, 1992

Bibliography

The Bible: Authorized King James Version, Oxford University Press, Oxford (1997 Edition).

Bodhi, Bhikkhu (editor); *In the Buddha's Words: An Anthology of Discourses from the Pāli Canon*, Wisdom Publications, Boston (2005).

Huang, Chichung; *The Analects of Confucius – A Literal Translation with an Introduction and Notes*, Oxford University Press, Oxford (1997).

Dawood, N.J.; *The Koran: Translated with Notes*, Penguin Books, London (Fifth Revised Edition, 1990 as reprinted with minor revisions 2003).

Donne, John (Rivers Scott editor); *No man is an island – A selection from the prose of John Donne,* The Folio Society, London, England (1997) (originally published 1624).

Horne, Charles F.; *The Rig-Veda The Oldest Aryan Book 2000-1000 B.C.* extracted from *Sacred Books and Early Literature of the East: India and Brahmanism*, Kessinger Publishings (originally published 1917).

Ibrahim, Ezzeddin and Johnson-Davies, Denys (Translators); *An-Nawawi's Forty Hadith: An Anthology of the Sayings of the Prophet Muhammad*, The Islamic Text Society, Cambridge (1997).

Kennedy, Robert F.; *Day of Affirmation Address*, University of Capetown, Capetown, South Africa (June 6, 1966).

Krishnaraj, Veeraswamy; *The Bhagavad-Gita – Translation and Commentary*, Writers Club Press, Lincoln (2002).

Locke, John; *Two Treatises of Government* and *A Letter Concerning Toleration*, Digireads.com Publishing, Stilwell, Kansas (2005) (first published 1690).

Marx, Karl; *Das Kapital: A Critique of Political Economy*, Regnery Publishing, Inc., Washington, D.C. (2000) (first published 1885).

Marx, Karl and Engels, Friederich; *The Communist Manifesto*, Oxford University Press, Oxford (1992) (first published 1848).

Mill, John Stuart; *On Liberty*, The Bobbs-Merrill Company, Inc., Indianapolis (1956) (first published 1859).

Rousseau, Jean-Jacques; *The Social Contract*, Penguin Books, London (1968) (translated by Maurice Cranston) (originally published 1762).

The Torah: The Five Books Of Moses, The Jewish Publication Society, Philadelphia (Third Edition, 1992).

Smith, Adam; *The Wealth of Nations*, Bantam Dell, New York (2003) (originally published in 1776).

Tzu, Lao; *Tao te ching*, Wordsworth Classics of World Literature, Ware, Hertfordshire (1997) (translated by Arthur Waley).

The Upanishads, Penguin Books, London (1965).

About The Author

Phil Thompson lives near Toronto, Canada. He is a business lawyer by trade. Phil is married with four grown children.

About The Publisher

Ancaster-based Manor House Publishing Inc. was founded in 1998 and has established itself as a leading publisher of primarily Canadian works of fiction and non-fiction. Manor House takes pride in publishing unusual and thought-provoking works, including many titles by first-time authors.

Many Prophets, One Wisdom

Manor House
905-648-2193
www.manor-house.biz

www.ingramcontent.com/pod-product-compliance
Lightning Source LLC
Chambersburg PA
CBHW030105240426
43661CB00001B/17